3 Hours

33 Minutes

In

Heaven

By Regan Forston C. M. H.

This book is nonfiction. Names of some of the people mentioned in this book have been changed to protect their privacy.

Visit my website at www.VisitTheAfterlife.com

First Printing: February 2020

Edited by: Patricia Cohn

Cover by: Sterling Hunter

ISBN- 978-0-578-63891-1

Forward

Patricia Cohn edited this book. She tirelessly worked on my book for three months, having me do four rewrites. I am eternally grateful for her helping me bring this book to press.

Table of Contents

· First Acting Jobs · Why Hollywood? · Soul Recognition

· Home Free

· Watching the Unthinkable · Murder at KFC · Torture · Handwriting Analysis Booth

· Killing Hundreds · Today, He Would Kill Himself · Left for Dead · Suicide by Rope

· Mexico's Dark Side · Lorena, Ex Cartel Boss · Gang Revenge

· An Evil Man · American Fugitives

· The Debutant Coyote · Killed by Chemo · Shot in the Leg

· Booted out of Mexico

· Validity of the Research · What We Know so Far · The Seven Stations that LBL Clients Visit. 1. The Soul Group 2. The Council of Elders 3. The Library 4. Next Life Selection Room 5. Places of Recreation 6. The Place of Rejuvenation 7. The Place of Higher Learning

 Few Things We Found in Our Research

As For Me -Making Sense of It All

Introduction

I am one of the 200+ certified therapists from the Newton Institute who are continuing the research of Michael Newton, who passed away in 2016. Over 50 years ago, Michael discovered that each one of us has a built-in God Switch, allowing us to communicate directly with Heaven. In a deeply relaxed state, people easily access this switch and can transcend their physical bodies, spending hours exploring Heaven just like I did two years ago.

We at the Newton Institute want the world to know about this process, and I'm writing this book, hoping it will inspire you to have this life-altering experience for yourself. The 50,000+ people that have had this experience to date have helped us discover what happens at death, where we all go, and what we do when we get there. Yes, Heaven is real.

This book is about my personal life's journey leading up to my 3 hours 33 minutes in Heaven and how God prepared and guided me to be a Life Between Lives therapist. Some of what you read may be hard to believe, but I assure you it is all real. I have changed the names of some of my clients to protect their privacy.

Chapter 1

Setting the Stage

The two best days of your life are when you are born, and the day
you discover what your mission is.   *Soul Getty*

Experiencing Heaven has been the highlight of my life. I'm still
integrating what I learned two years after this miraculous event.
When I was in Heaven, a Guide gave me this prayer to say upon
awakening each day. "Bless this day and those I serve as I keep one
foot in Heaven, and one foot planted firmly on Earth to help me
accomplish my life's mission."

Imagine visiting Heaven in a controlled environment and staying
there for hours with the help of a facilitator. As part of my training
to become a certified Life Between Lives therapist, I went to Heaven
and back. A trained facilitator guided me to a deep state of
relaxation, the point just before sleep. I slipped into a super-
conscious state, allowing me to visit the place a person goes between
lives. It was glorious.

The thousands of people who have had this experience have come
from every spiritual path imaginable. Glimpses of Heaven and
interaction with Angels, Guides, etc. have been documented for ages
across most cultures. The Bible references such things dozens of
times. People reported having glimpses of Heaven during "near-
death experiences," like St Paul when he was being stoned and saw
the highest Heaven. Others saw Heaven in visions, dreams, and

meditation. These events have changed people's lives, even though they lasted just a few seconds or minutes.

Our cultural conditioning can sometimes cause us to get hung up on words. There are many names for God and the celestial beings who reside in Heaven, so if the words I use for spiritual descriptions don't resonate with you, please change them to what feels right for you.

It's not my intention to preach to you or attempt to change your beliefs. We are all on our own unique individual life path, seeking awareness of the Divine. New research has unveiled information that was not available when most of us formed our concept of Heaven, so please keep that in mind as I share these new discoveries with you. How you assimilate, this information is up to you. I hope it will enhance your view of God and Heaven like it has mine. As you will see, truth and love are available to all with a loving heart.

Facing My Past Sins

My family and friends and have described me as an honest, kind, and compassionate man, willing to go the extra mile to help everyone, even strangers. I humbly receive this, but I wasn't always this way. When I've shared my past with clients and friends, they'd often say they can't even imagine I was ever like what I described.

I learned in Heaven that we often bad before we are good. We are selfish on our journey to selflessness; it seems to be the nature of Soul. We all miss the mark sometimes. I have never felt I was an evil man, but for sure, I have been a good man behaving badly at times. I know the mistakes I've made in this life and the people I've harmed, but what havoc have I caused in my other lives on my way to self-realization? There has always been a part of me afraid to open that door. Here is what happened on my way to Heaven.

I'm floating out in space and looking down at Earth, feeling free and at peace. Suddenly, I feel a tugging, like I'm being pulled backward up a slide. A split second later, I found myself in a disturbing scene from a past life.

From a slightly raised vantage point, I'm saddled to a spirited white horse overseeing a gruesome scene unfolding before me. My name was Celius, and I was a Roman soldier in charge of putting down what Caesar deemed a threat to Rome. Before me were rows of men hanging from crosses in various stages of dying; these men were fanatical, trouble-making Jews. My orders were to crucify them. As Celius, I felt justified. I was a loyal soldier and did what had to be done.

I wasn't emotionally prepared for this experience. The feelings I had of sadness, shame, and remorse as I witnessed this as Regan were unbearable. As these feelings erupted, another part of me emerged, calming me down. I guess it was my "higher self." If not, it was a soothing voice from an angel or a guide. Whoever it was, said I would soon know why I was being shown that life.

When I regained my composure, I saw more of my life as Celius and the remorse I felt as I died for the horrible things I had done in the name of Caesar. I left the body of Celius, and after a few roadblocks, Rebazar, a master who had taught me in my dreams, appeared and escorted me to Heaven.

As you will read, I saw another life where I was a Catholic monk, martyred for my beliefs. I can still feel the thump of the three arrows that pierced my chest. I wonder if that was payback, my karma for what I did as Celius.

As I write this, a recent client flashes across my mind. He was a young man who came to me for a past life regression. When he went through the tunnel into the light to a significant event in a previous life, he looked down at his feet and began to cry. He yelled NAILS! He found himself being crucified. I wonder if it was me as Celius who killed him.

The emotions I felt as I experienced my past life as Celius were intense but necessary for awakening to a deeper meaning of life. You will see that my sins in this life and past lives were many. You will also see me come face-to-face with scores of people I've harmed and witness the power of redemption.

Chapter 2

The God Switch

W hat if we all could communicate freely with Him? What if we all have a "God Switch," enabling two-way communication between Heaven and Earth?

I'm excited to tell you we've discovered that everyone has this heavenly, metaphysical switch within them. That means anyone can now visit Heaven. When I heard this, I was in disbelief, but having been there, I know it to be true.

Many people throughout history seemed to have had this ability, such as 15th-century saints Teresa of Avila and John of the Cross. Their writings have been preserved and published.

For example, St. Teresa documented how she found herself out of her body and in the direct presence of Jesus. Talking face-to-face, He told her where to establish new convents. Throughout history, people from many faiths have had the same ability to get help and guidance from Heaven.

My Catholic conditioning taught me that only saints were worthy of having spiritual experiences. The truth is, we can all communicate with Heaven. The researchers at the Newton Institute have been proving this for over 40 years.

How would your life be different if you could communicate directly with Heaven? Wouldn't life be more joyous if you knew for sure what your life's purpose was? If you understood what happens after death, wouldn't you find it easier to deal with the loss of loved ones? Learning why your nemesis is making your life so challenging would make it easier to deal with them, too, wouldn't it? With all this knowledge and perspective, don't you think you'd be more kind, selfless, and more apt to make better decisions in your life?

Here are some things you can do when visiting Heaven:

- Ask questions and get answers about your current life

- Visit past lives to see where you've been and the lessons you learned

- Talk to loved ones who have passed away

- Talk to people alive in your current life

- Understand why you incarnated on Earth

- Learn what your life's mission is

- Get proof for yourself of God's existence

- Find out if there is a Hell

- Gain an understanding of why bad things happen to good people

- Bring to light the reasons certain people are in your life

- Clarify who your soul mate is

- Understand what spiritual teaching or religion is best for you

- Have a conversation with Jesus or Mohammed or, your assigned Guide

- Discover who your Guide or Angel is.

- Get a spiritual or physical healing

What questions would you like to ask if you visited Heaven? Here is a great idea; buy a notebook today and make a list of what you would ask if you visited Heaven.

Then note the cast of characters in your life and write a sentence or two about your interaction with each of them. These will be the people that bring joy to your life and the ones who are a challenge to be around. In Heaven, we exist as energy beings. Research shows that, when souls incarnate in this world, they don't infuse their new bodies with all of their soul energy. That means that part of them is also in Heaven. So, when you're visiting Heaven, not only can you visit loved ones who have passed on, but you can have conversations with people who are alive and part of your current life. Can you imagine asking one of your antagonists why they are making your life so difficult? You can do this and amazingly, they will answer you lovingly and respectfully.

There is a part of you that lives in Heaven, your 'higher self.' Albeit hard to grasp, when I had my experience in Heaven, there was a point when I merged with my higher self. I felt the Wisdom of Solomon, like a better version of myself, and spoke in third person, giving myself advice about my current life.

Just like me, you have this God Switch and can activate it in your Life Between Lives session. Any doubts you may have about this process will vanish when you have the experience for yourself.

Chapter 3

Faith vs. Personal Experience

I have been a seeker, and I still am, but I stopped asking the books and the stars. I started listening to the teaching of my Soul.
Rumi

There are two basic ways to experience the love of God, through blind faith and personal experience. One is physical, the other metaphysical. I find it interesting that both schools of thought exist within each of the major religions.

Blind faith means that a person limits their beliefs to what is written in their holy scriptures. They accept nothing that adds or subtracts from the written word. People who believe that the way to know God is through personal experience believe that the holy scriptures are just the starting point to awaken a seeker to his inner self. With the awareness that the Kingdom of God is within, the seeker establishes a direct connection with the true essence of God. Through dreams, visions, intuitions, miracles, and soul travel, one gains a deeper understanding of the Scriptures. With this new knowledge, a person can navigate the difficulties of this life more easily. Think of it this way — two mechanics are working in the same shop. One has a basic toolkit, and the other has a tool kit with many specialty tools. Who do you think will have an easier time repairing the cars? Establishing a metaphysical, inner connection gives you access to these specialty tools.

Both schools of thought seem to exist side-by-side in most of the major religions. What happens in most cases is a blending of the two beliefs, leaving the religions somewhere in the middle in their understanding of God. Looking at it another way, within each religion, there are conservatives, liberals, and moderates. The list below shows the conservative side versus the more experiential side of each major religion.

Christianity and Gnosticism

Judaism and Kabbalah

Hinduism and Sikhism

Islam and Sufism

Each person walks their unique path to God. You get to choose whether you want to believe in God by having faith in the written word or by having both the written word and personal, metaphysical, spiritual experiences. I have chosen the latter.

Chapter 4

Reincarnation

"Condemnation without investigation is the height of ignorance."

Einstein

I find it interesting that the experiential sides of all major religions believe in reincarnation. Let's talk about that for a minute. How can reincarnation be a "woo woo" concept when 40% of the world believe in it? In a survey taken by CBS News, surprisingly, 25% of Christians reported that reincarnation is a possibility.

There are many documented cases of people who had a past life regression and, upon doing some research, found proof of themselves in that past life. For over 40 years, the University of Virginia has been researching children who remember past lives and compiled some very compelling proof. The children remembered their lives in remarkable detail, and upon diligent investigation, were proven to be correct.

Here is another way to look at reincarnation. "I have not lived many lives; rather, I have lived one life with many bodies."

If you really want to understand reincarnation, doesn't it make sense to do your own research? There are hundreds of books on the subject. For a direct experience, find a well-regarded past life regressionist in your area and book a session.

In my therapy practice, I am continually amazed at how easy it is for my clients to experience a past life. As a researcher, I keep meticulous records and can tell you that 82% are successful on the first try. The success rate is 94% on the second attempt.

I don't feel that God cares one way or the other if you believe you have lived before. It is not a requisite for being loved by Him or getting to Heaven. Reincarnation illuminates that your journey to becoming more Godlike is a longer process than you imagined.

Chapter 5

Death

I was four years old, and I can remember the outside of the Catholic Church we attended every Sunday, but not the inside except for the sickening smell of incense that burned my eyes. Somehow, I knew more about the Lutheran Church that was 50 feet from my house. My mother told me that Lutherans differed from us. I sat on the front porch, watching them coming and going from the church, and I couldn't see any difference.

The only Lutheran I knew was the hunchback, church janitor, who had befriended my sister and I. Whenever he walked down the alley towards the church, I'd rush to get my sister, and we'd wait for him. His back was so curved that his head pointed to the ground. He walked slowly and deliberately, looking upward every few steps to see where he was going. Whenever he saw us, a shy smile emerged from his wrinkly face, and he'd reach into his denim overalls and give us a piece of Doublemint gum. He never said a word, just smiled, and then disappeared into the side door of the empty church. He was our friend.

One day, my father sat my sister and me down to tell us that the janitor had died. It confused me. No one had told me about death.

My father walked me down to his house to attend his wake, and I saw him lying in a box at the back of the room. A light was shining on him, and he looked like he was asleep but somehow different. It was his stillness that I felt, like I was looking at a slab of fish on the kitchen counter that Mom defrosted, stiff, cold, and motionless. I followed my father's lead, knelt, and made the sign of the cross. I noticed that he didn't look crooked anymore.

The only time I can remember my father holding my hand was on the walk back home. My father said not to worry about him because he was in Heaven now. I asked, "What is Heaven?"

My First Out of Body Experience

I lived in Richmond, Indiana, in an old two-story house with creaky wooden stairs. My bedroom was upstairs, all the way at the end of the hall.

I awoke one night, startled to find myself on the ceiling looking down at my body. A second later, I'm back in my body and could see a ball of energy on the ceiling. Then I'm up on the ceiling again, looking back at my body. As I reentered my body the second time, I jumped up and ran into my parent's room and shook my father awake. I couldn't put into words what had happened. He took me back to my room, turned on the lights, checking the closet, and under the bed, and lovingly assured me I was safe. He said my imagination had gotten the best of me.

I found myself out of my body the next night and the night after. One night, I was so afraid to fall asleep I tried sitting up in bed and propping my eyes open with my fingers, but eventually, they closed.

I was still sitting up when something woke me. I opened my eyes to find two men standing in the middle of my room. I wasn't afraid. Dressed in white, they stood there, smiling at me. I don't remember seeing their lips move, but I heard one of them say, "It's ok to go to sleep now." Calmly, I got under the covers and went back to sleep. After that, I was never afraid to go to sleep again.

Chapter 6

Catholic Indoctrination

I'**m in first grade at** St. Michael's in Indianapolis, and my indoctrination into the Catholic Church had begun. Well-meaning people were programing my young brain to believe that the Catholic faith is the one and only way to Heaven. The Pope is the closest guy to God, and he's infallible, never makes mistakes, and whatever he tells us it the absolute truth. Believing that was somehow comforting.

The nuns taught me there were two kinds of sins, mortal and venial. If you commit a mortal sin, you go to hell and burn forever. With a venial sin, you only burn for a little while. They weren't effective at delineating the differences between the two, so many times I wondered if I had just committed a mortal sin.

After school one day, I went across the street to Tommy's house, where we played army with little plastic soldiers in his sandbox. He had this cool rubber grenade that we filled with sand and threw at the enemy soldiers. His mom called him in for dinner, and I stayed in the sandbox and kept blowing up the enemy soldiers over and over with that cool grenade. I wished it was mine. The desire was so strong that I stole it.

As I walked across the street, pictures of hell flashed through my mind. I raced back and hurled the grenade back into the sandbox. I was relieved for a moment, but when I got home, I was stricken with fear. Even though I returned it, I had stolen it. Will I still burn in Hell? My Catholic programming was beginning to work.

Hanging Myself

A few weeks later, Tommy's mom saved my life. As she glanced out her kitchen window, she saw me standing on a chair with a noose around my neck under the rafters of my carport. I can still hear her screaming as she raced across the street.

No, I wasn't trying to kill myself over the guilt I felt about stealing the grenade. I had just watched a man get hung on a cowboy show on TV and was curious about what would happen. I guess I wasn't the smartest five-year-old on the block. Years later, in a past life recall, I watched as I threw a rope over a tree branch and hanged myself. I wonder if that buried past life memory had influenced me?

First Communion

As we were walking from our classrooms to the church to practice for our first communion, the girl in front of me told Sister Vigil that she had a friend who was a Protestant. Without missing a step, Sister said, "Your friend is a pagan and will go to Hell."

Later that day, we practiced sticking out our tongues to receive the body of Christ. I wondered what a body tastes like. I was a little disappointed that it was just a round small white wafer that tasted chalky. The same girl reached up and took the host out of her mouth to look at it. Sister slapped her across the face for touching the body of Christ. I wonder if that little girl is still a Catholic. The Church has evolved a lot since then, as we all have. So much of my indoctrination was rooted in blind faith and fear.

Chapter 7

Accessory After the Fact

Lots happened between 1955 and 1968. I attended Parochial schools throughout high school. My biggest sin to date was buying stolen car parts for my 1957 Corvette. I bought the car for $500 and then rebuilt the whole engine in my garage.

A boy who lived a few blocks away offered me two stolen racing tires. I knew they would make my Vette look awesome, so I bought them. Two days later, someone stole the tires from me. That didn't stop me from buying a stolen transmission a few weeks later from a friend at work. A week later, my car was stolen. The police found it totally stripped. I saw how karma works. When I transgressed, there was an immediate consequence.

I also noticed that when I hung around "bad" people, bad things happened. A few days after I bought the transmission, the police showed up at my work place. I heard them talking to my boss about my friend who had sold me the transmission. My heart sank. They got me, I thought. But a few minutes later, they drove away.

That night, it startled me to see my friend's face on the news as police were looking for him in connection to a murder. I found out that he and another acquaintance of mine were burglarizing a home in my neighborhood. When the owner walked in, they panicked, held her down, and killed her with a monkey wrench. They were each sentenced to 20 years in San Quentin. Years later, he was shot in the back, trying to escape. I heard he survived, and always wondered what happened to him after that.

"It's a Mystery"

I was a typical teenager, thinking only about cars, girls and things I wanted to buy. God was just a concept. I was a Catholic robot, following along with everybody else, not having a clue about what all these rituals meant. I was just going through the motions and doing what was expected of me.

Jesuit High School was great. I got an excellent education and liked the priests and brothers who taught me. They rarely discussed the Bible. The emphasis was on the Catechism of the Catholic Church, the principles we were supposed to live by. The priests were great about answering my questions about the rules of the Church, but when I asked anything about the Bible or posed a profound philosophical question, they didn't have a clue. The usual response I got was, "It's a mystery." If the priests don't have any answers, who does? The walls of my Catholic upbringing were showing cracks. I see now why most religions discourage the exploration of different beliefs. That's their way of keeping you in the fold. "God forbid" you discover there are other ways of viewing and understanding God. My blinders were about to come off, and my life was about to take a huge turn.

Expanding My Awareness

After graduating from high school, I enrolled in American River College, the first public school I ever attended. I discovered that there are other ways of looking at God. I learned the about agnosticism. That describes me, I thought.

One day, in my comparative religion class, the subject of reincarnation came up. I found it intriguing until the teacher said that in India, they believe that cows are the reincarnated souls of humans. I laughed along with the rest of the class.

Chapter 8

The Awakening

At age 24, I was happily married and had a 4-year-old son. I owned a new home in Sacramento, California, and had just started my own real estate company. I was still confused about God, so many questions and very few answers. God must have felt my frustration and decided it was time to wake me up.

The Cliff

Dreams… I don't remember ever dreaming. I was always told that dreams are meaningless, so I never gave them much attention. That was about to change.

During a dream one night, I woke up and kept dreaming. Strangely, I was aware I was asleep and aware that I was dreaming. The plane I was in crash-landed on a remote island, and only a few of us survived. For a moment, I was relieved to be alive. As I looked around at my surroundings, I sensed an evil presence. I screamed as this evil force chased me up a mountain, cornering me at the edge of a cliff.

I will die! I thought. Suddenly, a giant hand came up out of the clouds. Thank God I can jump into the hand to safety. But I didn't jump. I just stood there. Something deep inside told me I had to make a conscious, split-second decision to jump into the hand to safety or turn around and face the monster chasing me. I screamed, "I'm going to turn around!" As I began to turn, I woke up. I grabbed a piece of paper and wrote all I could remember about my dream. I shook my wife awake and told her what had just happened, "I think I just passed a test," some spiritual test, and I think it had something to do with facing my fears. Something shifted in me that night. The dream was the first I ever remembered and the first I ever wrote down. Looking back, I know it was a wake-up call from God. My search for God accelerated.

(Forty-Four years later, this dream would play a significant part in my experience in Heaven.)

Spiritual Path Finds Me

After receiving my "wake-up call," I became interested in anything and everything spiritual. I saw a tabloid magazine headline at the checkout counter in the supermarket that said, "How to Astral Travel." I didn't know what that was, but it stimulated some unexplored part of myself. Following the instructions, I laid down on the bedroom floor, closed my eyes, and tried to imagine myself floating up through my roof and into space. The instructions said that once in space, I would see a silver cord extending from me down to Earth; nothing happened.

A few weeks later, I was watching the Tom Snyder show while he was interviewing a man who talked about dreams, past lives, and soul travel. I was so intrigued I wrote down the name of his organization. The next day I was at the library researching Eckankar. There I was, researching something for the first time in my life. Something beyond myself was driving me.

I've been an Eckist for over 45 years now, and it has served me well. They taught me how to soul travel and how to have personal experiences with God. I learned the importance of dreams and how to recognize the inner guidance that God is always providing. This path has been a good fit for me. It is up to each of us to find the spiritual path that resonates with us. You may have already found yours.

I once facilitated a Life Between Lives session, and a client asked the teachers in Heaven what the best religion is; the answer he got was "the one you choose for yourself."

If the religion or spiritual path that you are following doesn't resonate with you or you've outgrown it, it's probably time to move on. If you feel good about the path you're on, immerse yourself in it.

The Importance of Dreams

Eckankar taught me a spiritual exercise to try on my own. It's simple; all I had to do was to sit quietly and sing Hu, (sung Huuuuuuuu), and watch the inner screen of my mind. The word HU is an ancient name for God and carries the highest vibration of any sound on earth. When sung, the vibration opens the door between here and the highest reality.

Excitedly, I began my inward journey into the unknown. I had hoped that singing the HU would give me an immediate Soul travel experience, but it didn't, that would come later. When I did this spiritual exercise, it always gave me a genuine sense of peace and calm, and that motivated me to continue.

Besides being taught how to soul travel, I learned the importance of dreams. I took some classes to understand the many types of dreams and how to differentiate between them. I started a dream journal, and a new adventure began and continues to this day.

I have learned to wake up in my dreams and analyze them while they are happening. Benevolent guides and teachers appear in my dreams, guiding and showing me how to be more selfless and kind. I even had a few dreams that showed me vignettes of my future. If I hadn't written them in my dream journal, I would have forgotten them and lost the message. I now had a powerful tool to facilitate my spiritual unfoldment.

Chapter 9

Yellow Sky & Giant Oak Trees Dream

When we sleep, the critical part of our mind relaxes, opening up the opportunity for soul travel. I was about to have an out-of-body experience that would stay with me for the rest of my life.

As a real estate broker, I sold undivided interests in a 5,000-acre ranch on the Northern California border. My wife and I bought one for ourselves. Having an undivided interest means that everyone equally owns the land and everything on it. It was a stunning and gorgeous place on the Klamath River with salmon and steelhead fishing, 50 horses, buffalo, and it backed up to a million acres of National Forest. I remember killing a rattlesnake that almost bit me and digging out two ounces of gold in one of the creeks running through the property.

One night, instead of staying in the ranch bunkhouse, we pitched a tent next to the creek that ran through the property. I had been experimenting with singing the HU in my contemplation exercises for weeks before going to bed. I got into my sleeping bag, closed my eyes, and sang the HU as I drifted off to sleep.

I awoke and found myself in another world, hovering about 50 feet off the ground. I had never seen a place more beautiful than this. The skies were yellow, and there were rolling meadows of wheat-colored grass as far as I could see. The most magnificent part of the scene was the giant trees sprinkled across the meadows. They were massive, similar to oak trees on earth but thicker and darker. They were majestic and emanated a powerful positive energy that I felt to the core of my being. As I hovered over this scene, I felt buckets of love being poured over me. I have never felt as loved as I did at the moment. This must be Heaven, I thought.

Then I realized I was seeing all this from a 360-degree viewpoint. How could this be? "I'm out of my body! I did it! I'm soul traveling!" Instantly, I found myself back in my body. As I lay there reliving what had just happened, I felt profound peacefulness, and any fear of death vanished. I now knew that Heaven is real and that I am more than this physical body and mind. I hoped that I could return to that place of peace and love. I would never look at the world in the same way.

I refer to this experience as the "Yellow Sky and Giant Oak Tree Dream." Years later, a miracle would happen in my life to show me that this wasn't my imagination.

Chapter 10

Miracle in Saint Louis

People in our lives are a mirror for us, reflecting our faults. In my 20s, I smashed the mirror that my first wife held up. Forty years later, I'm still picking up the pieces. It was then that I reached my low point, my bottom. For the first time, I reached out to God and asked him for help. I had realized, I can't do this alone. As you will read, the help came instantly and has continued to this day. I've been guided to earthly processes and teachers in my outer life and been getting help through dreams, visions, and out-of-body experiences in my inner life. I have slowly emerged from being selfish to selfless. Don't get me wrong, I still have occasion to screw up, but I am always getting better.

It's 1979, five years since I had my out-of-body experience with the giant oaks and yellow sky. These experiences have become a common occurrence, usually one or two significant events a year.

With all these spiritual experiences, one might think I would have become a saint, but that's not how it works. Raising your consciousness happens in a slow but steady process. I still had personal issues of anger and addiction. Some days I thought God had abandoned me, but I kept doing my spiritual exercises, and a miracle would happen to put me right back on track.

Pick your addiction, drugs, sex, eating, gambling, shopping, alcohol, etc. Any one of these can bring you to your knees. Mine did just that at age 29. The guilt, the shame, the self-loathing, I just couldn't stand it any longer. I confessed everything to my wife, and it devastated her.

A few days later, we were on a plane heading to a church camp out at Beaver Bend State Park in Oklahoma. On a layover in Saint Louis, the second leg of our flight got canceled due to some mechanical failure. The airline put us up in a hotel nearby for the night. My wife had not said a word to me in three days, and I could visibly see her emotional pain. As she laid on the bed in our hotel room, I walked outside and sat on the steps, hating myself for causing the woman I loved so much pain. What now? I still had the addiction and knew I was helpless to control it. My sadness and fear were overwhelming. I was experiencing the lowest point of my life; I cried out loud. "God, I can't do this. Help me! Please! Please!" Feeling defeated, I walked back to the room, laid beside her, sang the HU inwardly, and silently cried myself to sleep.

I woke up in a dream and found myself in an operating room lying flat on my back, with a sheet up to my neck. A moment later, the operating room door swung open, and a smiling doctor rushed to my side. He was wearing blue scrubs as they wear in the operating room, and only his eyes were visible. As our eyes met, I recognized him as an Eck Master. He smiled at me with his bright blue, soulful eyes as if to say, "It's all right, I love you." Then the doors flew open again, and four more doctors rushed in. They were also Eck Masters and looked at me the same loving way. Their caring and light-hearted smiles comforted me.

They encircled me and began to walk clockwise around me, kissing every inch of the edges of my body. When I awoke the next morning, I could feel my addiction was gone. I felt light and free and happy. My addiction has never returned. My inner connection with these benevolent teachers has continued to grow.

Chapter 11

My Life Flips 180*

I've become more attuned to the whispers of soul. I know I am not alone and have benevolent beings in Heaven watching over me. They communicate with me primarily through dreams, visions, and small miracles. I often use my intuition to decipher what they are trying to convey to me and how it applies to my life. My inner ears and intuition have become more and more adept.

I'm a Ventriloquist

So, here I am, 29 years old, a successful real estate broker, and I have a dream one night that will cause my life to go in a completely different direction. I dreamt I was a ventriloquist. The dream was so powerful that the next day I found myself at the library researching ventriloquism. I felt a gentle hand was pushing me along, and all I could do was surrender and glide along with it. I had never thought of being a ventriloquist before. This was absolutely nuts!

I was surprised that there was a National Association of Ventriloquists that offered a year-long home study course. I ordered it, bought a ventriloquist puppet, a dog I named Harvey. I was off and running into a whole new career.

A year later, I was brave enough to book a school assembly show for 1st through 6th graders. I couldn't believe how hard the kids and the teachers laughed. Harvey was a hit, and I was hooked.

Clown School

About six months later, out of the blue, my wife announced that she wanted to go to clown school. We went together. Two years later, we were performing all over the West Coast at fairs, malls, and schools. Six years later, I was teaching at Clown Summer School at the University of Wisconsin and then at the University of Michigan. I was a proficient magician, stilt walker, and mime.

Corporate Comedian & Fake Motivational Speaker

A few years later, my career shifted and I became a corporate comedian and a fake motivational speaker, performing in three countries and 37 states. A highlight was performing at the Aladdin Theatre for the Performing Arts in Las Vegas for 5,000 people. Harvey (my talking dog) and I ended the show singing with an orchestra and getting a standing ovation. The laughter, the love, and joy I received that day were overwhelming.

Once, in a vision, a guide showed me a place in Heaven where comedy originates. From that day on, I've been able to write my comedy shows effortlessly. Developing a sense of humor has been one of the biggest lessons of this life.

I was grateful I listened to my inner guidance because the next 30 years were a blast. Halfway through my performing career, I realized God led me to be a comedian because I didn't have a sense of humor. But I do now!

Chapter 12

How About a Burning Bush?

Whenever a soul travel event occurred, it was always monumental. So much so, I've never forgotten them and the significance they have played in my life. Even though these spiritual experiences had changed my life, small whisperings of doubt bothered me. Maybe I just have an overactive imagination?

Why couldn't I just accept that I was born with both a physical and metaphysical reality and that the combination of them is who I am? I longed for hard evidence that would convince me these inner experiences were real and valid? Teasingly I asked God, "How about a burning bush or something?" He must have smiled and said, OK.

The Columbia Storyteller

A few weeks after my whimsical request for a burning bush, I booked my Comedy Magic show at the Calaveras County Fair, known for holding the National Frog Jumping contest every year.

Remember my first significant out-of-body experience with the Yellow Sky and Giant Oak trees? The one that proved to me I was more than a physical body and that there really is a Heaven?

I shared the stage with The Columbia Story Teller. Carl was his name, and he dressed like an old miner, wearing clothes from the

1800s. He was thin, about 50 years old, and had a long grey beard. Just being around him made me feel like I was living in the Gold Rush era. He was a docent at Columbia State Park, working in the blacksmith shop and conducting tours down into the old gold mine. He was a great storyteller, and people liked his show as he had a way of bringing his stories to life.

He was a fascinating character. Ten years earlier, he was a powerful figure in the corporate world in San Francisco. He invented a holographic camera that was way ahead of its time. A major camera company told him how excited they were about it and offered a lot of money for his invention. They took his invention and destroyed it. He said he was naïve and couldn't believe that they didn't want to have the world know about his device. He became so distraught and angry at the corruption of corporate America that he dropped out of society.

He moved to the foothills of the Sierra Mountains, became a gold miner, working a spot on the Stanislaus River. He would often work in the nude and became the talk of the town. A few years later, he met his wife and took his current job as a storyteller for the park. We became friends, and, a few weeks after the fair, my wife and I drove up to visit him and his wife at their quaint little cottage nestled in the woods on the edge of the State Park.

We all had a great weekend and made plans to see each other again. As we were saying goodbye the next morning and getting into the car, I felt Carl's hand on my shoulder. He said, "You might think what I am about to ask you is strange, but I feel I need to ask you something." About what, I said. About your dream, he said. I had never mentioned any dream or talked about my spiritual beliefs with him. Instantly, I said, "What color was the sky?" "Yellow," he said.

"What was I looking at?" "The Giant Oak Trees," he said. My knees buckled, and I leaned against the car. He invited me to come back into the house. I sat down, still in disbelief, wondering how he knew about a dream I had 13 years ago. And how did I know instantly what dream he was asking me about?

Carl continued, "Have you had the second part of the dream?" I said, "I don't know. What is the second part?" He said he couldn't tell me but that I'd know when I had it.

Carl told me he was a descendant of the ancient Order of the Magi, and he seemed to be the keeper of this spiritual dream. A few months ago, a stranger on vacation from another country approached him after his storytelling in the blacksmith shop. Looking a bit embarrassed, the stranger asked, are you the person I'm supposed to tell my dream to; the dream with the yellow sky and magnificent trees? Carl said this had happened many times over his lifetime. He can't explain why, but it has.

Driving home, I was floating on a cloud. Over the last 13 years, I wondered if the yellow sky giant oak tree dream was just my healthy imagination. Was I really out of my body? Was I really in Heaven? God gave me physical proof that what I dreamt was real. Since that day, I have never doubted the importance and significance of these inner spiritual experiences. I know now that I am both a physical and nonphysical being.

Chapter 13

First Past Life Experience

There are many ways a person can begin to understand that they have lived other lives. You can experience a past life during a dream, meditation, or déjà vu, to name a few. Hypnosis has been proven to be the best way, but I didn't know that at the time.

It had been 15 years since I awakened to my spiritual path. I sensed reincarnation was real, but I had seen no evidence of it in my life. My first past life experience was complicated and revealed itself over a period of a year, one piece at a time.

In the late 80s, I taught Clown School for two summers at the University of Wisconsin. The Dean of the Clown School at the University chose my wife and me to be Clown Ambassadors representing the United States at an International Clown Conference.

Clowns from 11 different countries arrived for the conference held in a 500-year-old castle in Edinburgh, Scotland. Between meetings, we performed at various theatres and schools in nearby towns. I found out slapstick humor is universal. Scottish kids laugh just as hard when they see you get a pie in the face as American kids do. The conference was a great success.

Afterward, we toured Scotland, Wales, and England. In Bath, England, our tour guide took us to see the Roman baths that were discovered under the city. Next to the baths, there was a pond dedicated to the Gods. Our guide explained how Roman soldiers etched prayer requests on coins and threw them into the pond. There were several recovered coins in a display case and one said, "Please kill Marcus. He stole my wife."

Abby Cathedral was the next stop on tour. As we approached the cathedral, I had an uneasy feeling in the pit of my stomach. I really didn't want to go in but didn't want to get separated from the group, so I overrode my feelings.

That eerie feeling came back when the docent told us hundreds of people were buried under the floors and in the walls of the church. The tour guide led us to another area of the church. In front of us was a row of narrow, straight-backed, wooden seats. The docent pointed to me and a few others and told us to sit in them. The chairs were on a platform above floor level, and the seats were so narrow from back to front that it forced me to sit up perfectly straight. The docent said these were the chairs the monks sat in eight times a day to pray. He joked that the chairs forced them to sit up straight so they wouldn't fall to sleep.

I must have closed my eyes during his spiel, I don't remember, but when I opened them I was shocked! I was all alone in the cathedral. Where is everyone? A moment ago, there were a hundred people here, and now they've vanished.

This made little sense. I tried to stand up but couldn't. I was catatonic and couldn't move a muscle. I began to panic. All I could move were my eyes. As I sat there motionless, a sudden calm came over me. A dream I had a few months ago flashed through my mind. I was a monk and tied to a post. I could feel the thump of arrows hitting my chest as I woke up from that dream. It had felt so real that I wrote it down in my journal.

Ok, God, what are You trying to tell me? A moment later, I could move my head slightly, but not my body. I nodded my head and BOOM! I flopped to the floor like a sack of potatoes. A minute later, my body started responding to my commands. I crawled to a small bench and laid my body lengthwise along it. Instinctively, I took my right elbow and thrust it behind my back. You could hear the sound echoing off the walls as my spine cracked into place all the way from my neck down. I got up and walked out of the cathedral as if nothing had happened. "God, you have my attention." I think you're showing me I was a monk in a past life, but why?

Divorce

A few months after returning from Europe in 1989, my wife and I mutually decided to divorce. I always thought marriage was forever, but somehow we both knew we needed to move on. God closed that door so that another one could open.

This is one very nice poem or saying or writing or whatever you wish to call it. It really puts things into perspective and makes you think about all sorts of past relationships.

Reason, Season, or a Lifetime

People come into your life for **a reason, a season or a lifetime**. When you figure out which one it is, you will know what to do for each person.

When someone is in your life for a **REASON**, it is usually to meet a need you have expressed. They have come to assist you through a difficulty; to provide you with guidance and support; to aid you physically, emotionally or spiritually. They may seem like a godsend, and they are. They are there for the reason you need them to be.

Then, without any wrongdoing on your part or at an inconvenient time, this person will say or do something to bring the relationship to an end. Sometimes they die. Sometimes they walk away. Sometimes they act up and force you to take a stand. What we must realize is that our need has been met, our desire fulfilled; their work is done. The prayer you sent up has been answered and now it is time to move on.

Some people come into your life for a **SEASON**, because your turn has come to share, grow or learn. They bring you an experience of peace or make you laugh. They may teach you something you have *never done. They usually give you an unbelievable amount of joy. Believe it. It is real. But only for a season.*

LIFETIME relationships teach you lifetime lessons; things you must build upon in order to have a solid emotional foundation. Your job is to accept the lesson, love the person, and put what you have learned to use in all other relationships and areas of your life. It is said that love is blind but friendship is clairvoyant.

-- Author Unknown

Starting Over

Starting over wasn't easy. For over 20 years, my wife and I had worked together, slept together, and did most everything together. I walked around in a fog, feeling like half a person for months.

I began dating again and met an absolute angel named Kathy. She was 40 years old and yearning for her prince charming. We instantly became friends. She was a joy to be with, but after four months, it became clear that our relationship wasn't headed towards marriage. That confused me since we had such a deep emotional connection. One hot summer night, as we floated in her pool, she looked at me with loving eyes and said, "Our relationship isn't going anywhere, is it." I held her and said, I don't know why, but I don't think so. We were sad and confused but knew it was best to part ways.

Take-Two

A few weeks later, I planned a month-long adventure that began by flying to the Eckankar Springtime Seminar in Chicago and then driving to Indianapolis to visit the homes where I grew up. From there, I'd drive to Michigan State University to check out Clown Summer Camp, where I was scheduled to teach the following year. Finally, I would visit relatives in Cincinnati for a few days and then attend the Annual Ventriloquist Convention in Kentucky. Little did I know what awaited me.

Miracles Abound in Chicago

The Marriott in downtown Chicago was bustling with people from 40 countries who had arrived for the spiritual seminar. During one of the breakout sessions, on the big screen, we were shown a famous painting of a Roman soldier holding a small baby over his shoulder. The facilitator asked us to close our eyes, go into contemplation, and see if this painting brought anything up on our inner vision. I got nothing, but walking out of the session, a woman approached me. She said that during the exercise, she had a vision about me, which she wrote on a piece of paper. Would you like to read it, she asked? Yes, I said and thanked her as she walked away.

In her vision, she saw me coming home from war to find that my wife had been killed, and my child survived. I grabbed my child and held her tight, vowing to protect her and all children for the rest of my life. As I read this, a deep sadness erupted from the core of my being. Overwhelmed with emotion, I began to weep. I was embarrassed as I had never cried in public. I tried to stop but was out of control, but then, a calmness came over me. I excused myself and rushed up to my hotel room. I sat in a chair, closed my eyes, and began singing the ancient name for God, HU. Within a minute, I was soul traveling back to another place and time. I was a Roman soldier coming home from war.

I saw my house on fire, and my wife laid face down in a pile of hay. As I turned her over and found she was dead, instantly, I realized that she's my sister Anne in this life. My child, where is my child? As I ran to my burning house, my precious little daughter was running toward me. I grabbed her and held her tight. Oh my God, I recognized this child is Kathy in my current life.

At that very instant, the phone rang in my hotel room, pulling me out of the vision. When I picked up the phone, the operator said, "You have a message from Kathy," whom I hadn't spoken to since we parted ways. I sank to the floor. Now I knew why Kathy and I were so close. The love for her as my daughter in that past life had carried over into this life.

I found out later that Kathy called hotels all over Chicago until she found me. Can you see how wonderful it is to have an inner connection with Heaven?

Visions are fascinating because you experience a split-screen of consciousness. In this vision, I found myself in the body of a soldier experiencing his emotions, and simultaneously, I'm Regan, aware that I'm sitting in a chair in my hotel room doing a spiritual exercise.

Another Past Life

Feeling happy from that experience, I went back into contemplation. Within a few minutes, I was out of my body again and looking down at a scene below. Standing on a hill was a monk preaching to about 100 people. That's me! Wow, that is me! It rang true to my core. I knew I was preaching against the corruption of the Catholic Church, and later, I was murdered because of it.

As I opened my eyes, I heard a distinct voice in my head say, "You were a friar." Hearing a voice, was I crazy? I have learned over the years that when God wants to reveal something pivotal to me, He comes from left field. This was real. For one, I had never heard a voice in my head, and two, I was not even familiar with the term friar. I've since learned monks sequester themselves, staying out of the public eye, and friars are monks out amongst the people, teaching. In my vision, I was preaching to a crowd of people. The dream I had when I was murdered as a monk and the experience in Bath England, when I was catatonic in the cathedral, rushed through my mind.

I had just experienced two past lives in less than an hour. God allowed me to see my life as the Roman soldier to show why I loved Kathy so much and also why she had come into my life. She helped me heal from my divorce, freeing me up to meet another woman who would become my wife. I still didn't know why I was being shown my life as a monk, but I trusted and continued to follow God's lead. More pieces to the monk puzzle were coming my way.

My roommate left the seminar early, so I looked around for a new roommate to share the cost of the room. A friend introduced me to Dory, who had come all the way from Alaska to attend the seminar. She told me she's full-blooded Eskimo and had been an Eckist for several years. We became fast friends, and on lunch break, we happened upon a bookstore. As we walked down an aisle, Dory noticed a book on the shelf, grabbed it, handed it to me, and said, "You should read this." With all that happened in the last few days, I looked toward Heaven and bought the book.

It's called *On the Breath of the Gods*, a book about what God's real intention is for marriage. I looked at the author and laughed. I knew this person from Sacramento and didn't even know she was an author. Now I knew I had to read this book.

The following morning, just before awakening, I had a dream about Dory. We were Indians, and I was consoling her because her child had just died. It felt so real.

As I opened my eyes and looked across to Dory's bed, she opened her eyes. I said Dory, you were in my dream. As I described the dream, Dory burst into tears, like I did the other night when I read the note from the woman who saw me as the Roman soldier. Dory came over and got in bed with me, and I held her until she stopped crying. A few hours later, she was on her way back to Alaska. I wonder about her sometimes and the connection we shared in a past life.

Chapter 14

Next Stop Indianapolis

I **was elated and floating** on air as I left the seminar in Chicago and headed towards Indianapolis. I stopped at a farm and bought a pint of fresh strawberries; sweet, juicy, I've never tasted better nor felt so happy and carefree as I drove down country roads tossing strawberry stems out the window. With all that had happened in the last few days, my connection with God was stronger than ever.

As I drove toward Indianapolis, memories of my childhood came flooding back. I remembered being a paperboy when I was nine and walking through fresh-fallen snow at five in the morning. I could still hear glass shattering when I threw a rock at a passing bus and the foul taste of my first cigarette at ten. I also remembered the "colored people only" signs on the public water fountains and how sad I felt when I heard a black man got beat up for dating a white woman.

One of my fondest memories was my father teaching me to golf when I was ten. My plan was to park near the golf course where we played for the first time and enjoy a round in the morning.

Screaming in the Rain

When I reached the golf course just after 1 a.m., it was pitch black and starting to rain. Too early for bed, I climbed into the backseat of my rental car, turned on the overhead light, and began to read *On the Breath of the Gods*, the book Dory had me buy.

When the author was a child, she had frequent visits from two guides. No one else could see them, but they were always there to protect her. The guides told her that one day they would help her write a book about God's real intention for marriage.

As I continued to read, the storm outside intensified. The book dove deep into male and female energies and explained how we're born with both, one being more dominant than the other. The problem is that we don't understand how important it is to develop the less dominant side of ourselves. I reread the paragraph, and then again, and for reasons I didn't understand, I began to scream; I mean, really scream. The energy was so intense that I jumped out of the car into the pouring rain. It began to thunder with flashes of lightning every few seconds. It wasn't like me to be so dramatic, but here I was, in the middle of the night, dancing and screaming on the green of the 18th hole in the middle of a thunderstorm. Something deeper than my conscious mind had found the Holy Grail. I now knew what was lacking in my spiritual development, and why Dory felt compelled to have me read this book. All my life, I had neglected the feminine side of myself.

Three days later, my mind was still racing on the way to Clown Camp at Michigan State. What did it all mean, and how am I going to develop my feminine side?

Chapter 15

Clown School Romance

I **arrived at Michigan State** early evening just in time for the welcome BBQ. My friend Millie, whom I met while I was teaching Clown School at the University of Wisconsin the summer before, ran to me and gave me a big hug. She said I want you to meet my friend, Connie. There was instant chemistry, and we talked long after everyone else had gone to bed. We finally decided to part ways and continue our conversation in the morning. I drifted off to sleep, thinking about her sweetness and beauty.

I had a premonition during a dream about Connie that night. I was driving her somewhere and couldn't control the car. She had me pull over and get in the back seat. Then, she got behind the wheel and took us the rest of the way. A week later, the premonition came true. I had hurt my back doing the Macarena at our clown dance and couldn't drive my car. It just so happened we both planned to visit relatives in Cincinnati after clown school. So, there I was in the back seat, resting my back as she drove us there.

I hurried to class in the morning, and when I opened the classroom door, Connie was right in front of me. She turned and smiled, and at that moment, a deep recognition stirred in me. I remember saying to myself, "It has started." We married 17 months later. Not only did I become a husband but also a stepfather to four beautiful, amazing daughters, ages 3 to 10. For the next ten years, they immersed me in feminine energy. I became a better listener, more compassionate, and even began expressing my feelings. It felt and still feels wonderful.

Full Circle

So what about monk stuff? How was all that related to my new family?

A few months later, I was chatting with a man I had just met, and he laughed with recognition when I shared my story about marrying a woman with four daughters. He said that as a monk in a former life, he had rejected anything feminine. He smiled and teased, "I recently got married and have three new daughters; I wonder if we were in the same monastery?" God has a sense of humor.

Now everything made sense. That was the final piece of my past life as a monk. I must have carried over from that life the belief that feminine energy is inferior. I'm happy to say that I learned the error of my ways.

In Heaven, I discovered that developing my feminine energy was one of my primary purposes in this lifetime.

I was beginning to appreciating the importance of understanding past lives. I'm a product of everything I have ever experienced in all lifetimes. I had gone from having no past life experiences to having visions of three in just two weeks, each revealing something I could apply to my present life.

Chapter 16
Personal Transformation

Yesterday I was clever, so I wanted to change the world. Today I am wise, so I am changing myself.

Rumi

Anger Management

I became aware I had anger issues in my first marriage, and unfortunately, they carried over into my second marriage. I did a poor job managing my emotions and lacked proper communication skills. My second wife, Connie, loved me enough to support me in getting help.

I conquered my anger issues immersing myself in three years of training via a program called *Man-Alive*. What a fantastic experience it was for my growth and emotional development. Over the next few years, I got back my self-respect and the respect of my wife and children. They seemed to change, as well. There's a bumper sticker I saw a few years ago that rings true. "My, how you've changed since I've changed."

New Warrior Training

I felt good about myself and the changes I'd made, but something was still lacking. Again, Connie came to my rescue. Her doctor highly recommended the *ManKind Project*, a national organization that helps men heal from emotional wounds and teaches them to live their lives with more love, purpose, and integrity. The *New Warrior* training helped me take a giant step forward in my emotional maturity. I came out of it more alive and authentic than I'd ever been. I had changed so much during those three days and, while I was afraid I would slip back into my old ways, I didn't.

A few months later, Connie met me at the door as I returned from work. She hugged me and said, "We need to talk." Oh my God, what have I done wrong, I thought? I was doing so well and liked myself, and was becoming the husband and father I always wanted to be.

I asked, have I done something wrong? She said no, but it's been difficult for the girls and I being around you because you're "too sugary." When you talk to us, you look us in the eye. It's hard for us to get used to your honesty and directness."

I laughed out loud in relief. I said, then you guys are just going to have to get used to the new me because I'm never going back to who I was before. Hearing that I'm "too sugary" was one of the nicest things I ever heard about myself. I was proud of my growth and development. To this day, I've never reverted to my old self and continue to strive to be honest, kind, and compassionate.

Chapter 17

Warrior Monk

The *ManKind Project* **offered another** program to anyone who had completed the New Warrior experience, called *Warrior Monk*. It's designed to inspire men and women to develop a mission statement for their lives and remove any obstacles in the way of achieving their goals. It's a spiritually based program open to men and women of all faiths and beliefs. I enthusiastically enrolled as I wanted to continue my transformation.

Twenty-five of us from all over the US arrived for the training. In the mix were a Rabbi, a Sufi mystic, a Buddhist monk, and Christians from several denominations. The remaining students were spiritual, with no ties to any faith. Each of us had chosen a spiritual path that spoke to us. During the seven-day program, we shared and practiced rituals of Christianity, Buddhism, Sufism, and Judaism. We sang Christian Gregorian Chants, meditated, danced as Whirling Dervishes, and learned Jewish customs.

Research from the afterlife teaches us that a soul will choose a religion or spiritual path that will best serve them in their mission, or teach them a spiritual principle they need to learn.

Every day was one of self-discovery. I fine-tuned my life's mission statement and made a list of things I needed to achieve to be successful. The facilitators had a miraculous way of allowing me to discover what physiological roadblocks were standing in my way. They helped me realize that I could not carry out my life's mission until I dared to face my shadow. I thanked God for sending me these amazing men. They created a safe place to confront myself and the courage to change.

Empowered by their gentle, yet powerful, guidance, I faced my shadow. I discovered and then struggled with my inner demons and came face-to-face with my self-esteem and self-worth issues. Shame and guilt surfaced from my past deeds. I also realized I had a fear of success. I will cherish forever the gifts I received that week. I now see my shadow as a big bully who, when challenged, runs away like a scared little mouse.

During transformational seminars, it takes me two or three days to let go of my false self and allow my true self to emerge. Lasting change can only occur when I'm embodying my true essence.

After dinner on day five, we were escorted to our rooms, handed a pitcher of water and asked to meditate until we heard a knock on the door. I was feeling so light and in harmony with my true self that it was easy for me to go into deep meditation. Within minutes, I had an inner vision of me playing a slot machine. I pulled the lever over and over, and nothing came out, but something within me said, keep pulling the lever. On the next pull, Jackpot! Out poured dozens of gold coins. I knew the message was, "if you keep going, you will have a huge payoff."

Hours went by, and I lost all sense of time. A few times, I came out of meditation; standing in the dark I sang Gregorian chants, spun myself around like a whirling dervish, and prayed out loud to God. Then I'd sit down and begin meditating again and soon lose all sense of being in a physical body.

At one point, a man I recognized appeared in my inner vision. He was standing about three feet away, just staring at me. Oh no, I thought, was this a man I had wronged in this life? As he stood there, I began to feel his emotional pain. I realized I was feeling the pain I had caused him. Then he disappeared, and another face appeared. It was a woman who I had said some unkind things to earlier in life. Now, I was feeling the pain I had caused her. Then another person and yet another showed up. It seemed to go on for hours. I saw and felt the pain of everyone I had hurt in this life. The sadness I felt for causing so much distress to so many people was a humbling experience.

Then I had another vision in a temple of some sort. They instructed me to go upstairs and someone would be there to help me. A beautiful angelic-looking woman greeted me and handed me a pure white robe. She smiled and told me to prepare for initiation.

A knock on my bedroom door interrupted the trance I was in, incredulously, 36 hours had passed! The staff assembled us and led us single file to the sanctuary instructing us to lie down. Once we were relaxed, the facilitator described the guided meditation we were about to experience. We would follow a path, ascending a mountain all the way to the top. When we reached the top, she would tell us to turn around and meet our true master. The music started and listening to her calm, angelic voice, up we went.

My mind started racing. Who was I going to see as my true master? Will it be the Mahanta (my inner guide that had been appearing to me in dreams and visions for years)? Maybe I will see Rebazar, another master who keeps showing up in my inner travels. Then I thought, what if I see Jesus and He tells me I have been off track all these years? I took a deep breath and prayed for God to show me my true teacher, whoever that might be.

We climbed higher and higher up the steep mountain, so many thoughts going through my mind. I felt relaxed yet anxious. Higher and higher, we were now reaching the summit. I walked the last few steps and stopped. The women's voice said, "Now, turn around and meet your true master." I turned around, and I was shocked! There, in front of me, smiling with the most loving smile, was ME. I began wailing like a baby, then noticed the entire room had simultaneously burst into tears.

Feeling spent, but elated, we quietly got up and walked to the dining room where the loving staff had prepared a nourishing late dinner. We ate in silence, contemplating what we had just experienced. To this day, I don't know what the others saw when they turned around and met their true master, but I think they saw the same thing that I did.

When I visited Heaven, I learned there is always part of us that lives there. That makes so much sense. Our "higher selves" are always in Heaven. As you will see in my account of my journey into Heaven, I merged with my higher self, whom I had come face to face with at the top of the mountain.

Chapter 18
Hollow Bones

IT was 1999, and I was proud of the man I was becoming and all the positive changes I had made in my life. I had developed a stronger "Inner Guidance," was loving myself and being kinder to all.

God kept offering up powerful transformational retreats for me to go. A few years had passed since I completed the *Warrior Monk* training, and because that was such a transformative experience, it didn't take long for me to say yes to *Hollow Bones*, the third and final program offered by the *ManKind Project*. This was a non-denominational training for men only, held at a Buddhist Monastery in the high mountains near Idyllwild California, about 400 miles south of my home in Sacramento. I was excited for my quest to begin.

Miracle of the Avocados

Three years ago, when I attended the New Warrior Training in the mountains near San Diego, they instructed us to bring food to share with six other men on the first evening. I had almost forgotten but remembered about an hour away from the training. I stopped and bought six avocados. I'm sure glad I did because the men who didn't were reprimanded in front of the group. In a tribe, if someone doesn't live up to their responsibilities, everyone else suffers. Several men went hungry that first night because a few didn't follow instructions.

So, here I am three years later, on my way to Idyllwild. This time there was no request to bring food, but I thought it would be a nice gesture to stop along the way and pick up something to share with the other men. I decided to buy avocados again.

As I neared the Monastery, I realized I was in the middle of nowhere, and there was no way I would find a grocery store. As I got higher into the mountains, it began to snow, so I gave up the idea of bringing avocados. Oh well, at least I had good intentions.

As I turned left onto a remote mountain road, guess what I saw? There, on the side of the road, in the snow, was a small pickup truck with a big sign reading "AVOCADOS."

My heart raced with the immediate recognition of yet another "God sighting" in my life. A little miracle created just for me. I felt that "bucket of love" moment, like I first experienced in the out-of-body, yellow sky, and giant oak trees dream. I was now certain this retreat would be another life-changing experience. Later in the week, we had the avocados for lunch, and they were great.

Snow Covered Monastery

The monastery was beautiful, nestled in a valley with mountains on three sides. The last snow of the season was draping its final few inches of white magic evenly over all that I could see. I heard the crunch of my footsteps as I walked toward the sanctuary.

At our welcoming dinner that evening, I met the 14 men I'd be sharing this experience with, some of whom traveled thousands of miles to get here. I was not alone in the quest for enlightenment.

The teachers were Buddhist monks, and Junpo was the head monk. He was an American who spent many years in Japan, becoming a Zen Buddhist Monk. I found out later about his "bad boy" past and how he had transformed himself in his 40s by studying Buddhism.

I didn't realize this was a silent retreat. Seven days without talking, this will be interesting, I thought. They assigned me a 6 x 10 cabin in the woods with a thin mat on the hardwood floor for sleeping. It was clean and cozy.

Each day, at 5 a.m., I was awakened by a gentle knock on my door. We did yoga from 5:30 to 7:00, and after breakfast began our meditation practice. We did nine hours a day of "open-eyed" meditation. That was not the kind of meditation I was used to. I usually meditated 3 or 4 times a week for 15 minutes with my eyes closed, sitting in a comfortable chair. That was easy; this was anything but easy. It took so much more concentration and discipline.

On the first day, after a few hours of meditating, Junpo announced we would now do walking meditation. Great, I thought, this will be easier. My back was already killing me and begging for relief. We lined up single file, and then Junpo said, "Take off your socks." We walked around the outside of the temple for an hour, barefoot in the snow. My feet were so cold I thought they'd fall off. This was so much harder than I imagined. I was beginning to wonder what I had gotten myself into.

On the second day, I had moments when I thought I couldn't go on. How the hell can these monks do this day after day, year after year? During open-eyed meditation, I cheated and closed my eyes for a moment. A second later, a loud reprimanding voice from across the room shouted WAKE UP! These monks were taskmasters.

I was coming to terms with how entitled and complacent I was. I intuitively knew my inner guidance was correct, and I was supposed to be there, so why was I fighting it? I realized my modus operandi hadn't changed. Like a metaphor for other aspects of my life, I'm always negative at first, resisting change, and then once my false-self drops away, I get with the program.

By the end of the third day, I found my stride, Yoga was awesome, and I could do some poses without falling over. I could walk barefoot in the snow and sit for hours without bitching to myself about my back. I dealt with it. I found that focusing on a leaf on a tree just outside the window made the open-eyed meditation easier.

It was three days since I had uttered a word, and I loved it. Silence really is golden. It's remarkable how we all become close without ever speaking a word. I think everyone would benefit from shutting up sometimes. The false self that I had arrived with was peeling away, and the real me starting to shine through.

The Big Stick

On the sixth day, I was in such a good place, feeling light and joyful. My outer, false self had slipped away. Why can't I always feel like this? I knew the training would be over soon and feared I would spread a fresh coat of plaster over the real me. But I also realized that this plaster would be much thinner than the old, allowing me to access my true self more easily.

In the afternoon, after another nourishing vegetarian lunch, we convened at the temple for our afternoon meditation session. About an hour into it, as I stared at my leaf outside the window, out of nowhere, intense feelings of anger started bubbling up. This is strange because I had no reason to feel angry about anything. I was as happy as I had ever been.

The feelings of anger began to escalate, seeping from every pore of my body. Intuitively, I realized I was leaching out all the unresolved anger that I had kept buried deep in my subconscious for decades or maybe even lifetimes. The feelings of anger were consuming me. I felt like screaming or smashing my hand through a wall. At the same time, I knew I wouldn't do so because I wasn't really angry.

I looked over at Junpo; he was reaching behind him to pick up a big stick. It was about four feet long, two inches wide and an inch thick. He slowly paced the circle stopping in front of John, two men away from me. Holding the rod high above his head, he looked into John's eyes. A few seconds passed; John nodded yes to Junpo and bent forward, his head almost touching the floor in front of him. Wham! Wham! Junpo slammed the big stick flat across John's back on either side of his spine. A moment later, unfazed, John raised himself and began to meditate again.

Junpo moved to the man next to me. He looked into his eyes, and the man shook his head no. As he approached me, my anger surged. When our eyes met, I silently screamed: "Ok, you motherfucker, hit me!!!" Come on, you bastard, Hit me! Hit me! Hit me! I bent over, and Wham! Wham! Wham! Wham! I felt the sting of the rod as it crashed down the length of my spine. Seconds later, I sat up. He was smiling at me with his dark soulful eyes, and I bowed to him. I felt my anger subside, like hot air escaping a balloon.

Kyosaku, or in English "encouragement stick," is used on a student when they're stuck. It shakes up the body to allow for a deeper state of awareness to occur. A monk has to have lots of training in the stick's use before they allow him to use it on anyone.

Flesh Burned From My Bones

I had released lifetimes of anger to fully prepare me for what happened next.

I'm sitting peacefully in my usual place, gazing out the window at my favorite leaf. My eyes are wide open, and then, I'm not there anymore. I'm in my home in Sacramento, and everyone I love is there. It must have been some kind of family celebration. My mother, father, my wife, some friends, all my children, and even my dog Mijo was there. Suddenly, I burst into flames. I saw my flesh burning from my bones; everyone was on fire. Mijo was enveloped in fire and split in half. There was no fear, no pain, and no emotion. I was just in the middle of the flames, watching it all happen. Then in an instant, I'm up in the air above my home watching the inferno.

Feeling an immense power emanating through my being, I thrust my right arm at my home, and it exploded. Empowered, I raced into space and surveyed the Earth below me. Again, I thrust my right arm at the Earth, and it exploded. What about the other planets, I thought? In quick succession, I thrust my right arm at each one, and they exploded. Now, even more empowered, I blasted toward the Sun, and like Superman; I crashed into the middle of it at a million miles an hour, exploding it into trillions of pieces. Then I surveyed the billions of galaxies, and all of creation, and I knew what I had to do. Using my unworldly power, I thrust both arms at all that exist, destroying it all.

Nirvana

Now, I'm in total darkness and silence, at peace, and immersed in love. I felt whole and complete, like I'm back to the beginning of me, my true essence. Is this Nirvana? My inner wisdom showed itself, and I knew what just happened. I had destroyed my personal universe for a whole new me to emerge.

I remembered that my physical body was back at the temple meditating and was sure the others would be standing over me, wondering what had happened. Instantly, I'm back. My eyes are still wide open, and I'm staring at my leaf outside the window. No one is even noticing me. I thought I'd been gone for a long time, but was I? To this day, I don't know if I was out of my body for an hour, or for only a second. This whole experience happened while I was sitting, staring at my leaf.

I was on such a high. I had experienced Nirvana, oneness with the Divine. I had destroyed my old self so that a new me could emerge, and I was eager to see who that would be?

Leaving the Mountain

On the last day of the training, we all met in the sanctuary after breakfast. Junpo asked us to make and commit to some personal vows, things that we promised to embody in our new lives. He encouraged us to shave our heads for the ceremony, as that would act as a constant reminder of our commitment to our vows.

No, I didn't have my head shaved even though half of the men did. Ben was a young man in his 20s who looked the way Jesus is portrayed in the movies. We all watched as his thick strands of shoulder-length hair fell in clumps to the floor. Even though I didn't shave my head, I have kept the vows I made that day.

For the graduation ceremony, Junpo had hired me to write and perform a custom comedy show based on all that went on during the training. Harvey, my talking dog, was a hit. People were laughing so hard, some with tears of laughter; what a wonderful way to complete this transformational week. I thanked God for the gift.

We all said our heartfelt goodbyes, wishing each other well. I wanted to savor this feeling, so I hung out until I was the only one left. As I stood marveling at the mountain behind the compound one last time, I had a crazy idea. In my mind, I had climbed it many times this past week. Why not do it for real? Overriding my fears of getting lost or hurt, up I went. The summit was about 2000 feet above me. A trail took me a quarter of the way up, and then I roughed it. It was challenging. At one point, I had to walk through snowdrifts and maneuver up steep embankments. I made it. The view at the top was breathtaking.

Feeling joy and gratefulness, I called my wife, Connie, to tell her how much I loved and missed her. I was so excited to share what I learned, but she was silent. When she spoke, I sensed something cold and distant in her voice. My heart sank. I feared the vision I had at the training about losing everything was about to unfold, and my life was about to come tumbling down.

Chapter 19
Painful Rebirth

Several months later, my wife asked for a divorce. In the blink of an eye, my life as I knew it dissolved. I lost my wife, my children, my business, and even my dog, Mijo.

What kept me from falling apart was remembering the out-of-body experience at the Hollow Bones training, foreshadowing that I would lose everything in order for a new me to be born. I surrendered into God's hands, trusting that things would work out for the best.

In the 20 years that have passed, I have been able to reconnect with my entire family in a much deeper, loving way. Ultimately, I lost nothing and gained everything.

The CD Miracle

I moved to Los Altos, a town south of San Francisco near San Jose. Through an online dating site, I met a fascinating woman from Russia named Ivana. In her childhood in Russia, she told me she had an apple tree outside her bedroom window on the second floor. She used to reach out and pick apples right off the tree. When it was movie night for the family, they didn't have popcorn; her mom would pick fresh apples. She said she loved apples.

We planned the first date but had to postpone it because her brother-in-law died. I felt compassion and wanted to do something nice for her. When I was mending my broken heart, I listened to some great CDs that helped me grieve, so I decided to give her some of them.

I was doing this from a genuine desire to help her cope with her sadness. It wasn't because I was trying to impress her; it was the kind thing to do. Along with the CDs, I also made her a gift basket, including an assortment of every apple I could find. Sitting in my car in front of her home, I sang the HU and prayed, asking God to let this music heal her. I placed the basket on her porch and drove away. I was resonating with my best self.

I remembered I'd seen an upholstery shop on the way to her home. I was considering having my leather steering wheel cover redone and thought this would be a good time to stop in and get an estimate. The parking lot at the upholstery shop was empty, and I saw a closed sign in the window. As I walked back to my car, I noticed the garage door on the other side was open. Maybe someone is there and would give me a quick estimate.

The man sitting at a table sewing leather smiled and said, "Come on in." What a nice guy. After a few minutes of small talk, I thanked him and started to leave. He said, wait a minute, I want to show you something. I followed him upstairs and as I reached the top step, I could see that he was taking me into his recording studio. He told me this is where the band he led practiced and proudly shared with me they had just finished recording a new CD. He reached into a drawer, pulled out a copy of the new CD, and handed it to me. "I want you to have this," he said. As he gave it to me, I had that half in, half out-of-body sensation that I get when I realize that God is communicating with me. What are the odds of giving someone a gift from your heart, and then a few minutes later, a random stranger gives you the same gift back? God was showing me I had done the right thing by giving Irina a CD just minutes before.

These "God Sightings" or "Waking Dreams," as I call them, have been constant in my life ever since the first days of turning my life over to Him. I always know when they're happening because of the body sensations that accompany them. I gave up calling them coincidences years ago.

Six Women and a Bride

Ivana and I fell in love, and I moved in with her. One weekend, I went by myself to a regional Eckankar seminar. One topic in the small groups was "Take a Chance on Love." I was still raw from my divorce and thought this topic would be perfect for me.

During the class, they asked us to close our eyes, sing the HU for a minute, and ask God to answer a personal question concerning love and relationships. I asked the inner master to give me clarity on my budding relationship with Ivana. I closed my eyes and instantly had a vision.

I'm sitting on a beach, and parading in front of me left to right, are three Eck Masters, with a woman on each arm. I counted six women in all. Right behind them, Rebazar, one of my inner guides, was escorting a woman on his left arm dressed in a wedding gown. A veil covered her face, and I could see blond hair peeking through. I heard a voice in my head, and it said, "That is all for this life."

The vision lasted all of 10 seconds, but startled me, especially hearing a voice in my head again. It showed me there would be other significant women in my life, women who I would love, but not be bound to until I met the woman behind the veil

I spent a year with Ivana, and we shared many special times. Just like Kathy, who I had met after my first divorce, they were the special souls who helped heal and prepare me for the next part of my journey. For that, I am grateful, and they will always hold a special place in my heart.

These visions I'm blessed with differ from a daydream or meditation. They have a different quality to them; they're powerful and unique and leave an indelible imprint on my mind. Fifteen years later, that vision manifested. I am now with the bride with the blond hair, my last meaningful relationship in this life.

Chapter 20
Hollywood Here I Come

You are not a drop in the ocean. You are the entire ocean in a drop.
                                                            Rumi

While performing in LA one weekend, I had another vision. Excited by what I saw, I couldn't ignore the message that I was to move to LA. The winds of change had become a common occurrence, and I felt called to be an actor. With 21 years 'experience performing and over 200 letters of recommendation from some of the biggest corporations in America, I thought getting acting jobs in Hollywood would be a cinch.

I moved into a loft in downtown LA, at the base of the 7th Street Bridge that spanned the cemented Los Angeles River. My loft was in a building where people paid their electricity bills in the 1920s. The smell of old red bricks filled the air, and I could "sock slide" on the polished cement floors. Every few hours, trains lumbered by leaving the scent of diesel and a fresh coat of black soot on my car. Barbed wire enclosed the compound, keeping the homeless and thieves out.

I had done an internet search and found that there had been 50 murders in the last year within a 5-mile radius of the loft. I knew I was supposed to be here, so it didn't faze me. I loved my new home.

At 2 a.m. on my first night, gunshots awakened me. Terrified, I sat up in bed and listened. Maybe the police were having a shootout with a gang? Five minutes went by, and nothing, no sirens, no yelling, only dead silence. What if it was a drive-by shooting, and a dead man was lying outside? Should I call the police?

A minute later -BAM- automatic gunfire. I crawled over to the window and peeked out, nothing there, just an eerie silence. Maybe moving here was a mistake; maybe my intuition was wrong.

Time passed, no sounds at all. I don't get it, shouldn't I hear police and ambulance sirens. Is it possible that even the police feel it is too dangerous to come here? Suddenly, more gunfire, hundreds of shots rang out. I ran over to my back door, away from the bullets and out into the courtyard. The guy who lived upstairs was casually climbing the stairs to his loft. I warned him about the shooting, and he began to laugh. Now I'm perplexed. He said, "Clearly, you're new here, aren't you. This is Hollywood, man; they're shooting a movie called *SWAT* on the bridge."

My first night in Hollywood confirmed this is the city of illusion, where nothing is as it seems.

First Acting Jobs

For months, I mailed resumes and visited agents' offices with no results. Well, I got one acting job if you can call it that. I was an extra in a movie where Jesus got hit by a bus, and my pay was lunch, a ham sandwich, and a coke. I was panicking as I burned through my savings. I remember closing my eyes and doing a spiritual exercise, asking God for some paying work. I promised Him I would take whatever work He sent my way.

A few days later, I responded to an ad seeking someone to be comic relief in a play called *Gay Times Requiem*. I didn't see how that would work but remembered I vowed I would accept anything He sent me. I auditioned, got the part, paying $500, and was told that I was the only straight guy in the production.

It was an intense story about the relationship between two men during the first outbreak of AIDS in the 80s. One of them was in so much physical and emotional pain that he begged his partner to kill him. His partner finally relented and suffocated him with a pillow. From backstage, I witnessed the audience as they wept.

What a powerful and eye-opening experience this was. I bonded with all of the men, and the experience allowed me to let go of my religious conditioning about homosexuality and brought me one step further in my spiritual awakening. The play was a great success and held over an extra weekend. My career as an actor had begun.

The research shows us that in Heaven, we are beings of energy. When a soul decides to have human experiences, it chooses to be either male or female, depending on which sex is more suited to its mission. In several case studies, a few souls purposely decided to be gay to learn how to deal with discrimination. In Heaven, we are a blend of male and female energy. Lots of clients report seeing souls there as androgynous.

During my 12 years in Hollywood, I was cast in lead roles in 35 short and independent films, and I worked as an extra on lots of major films. I worked next to Leonardo DiCaprio twice, once on the Queen Mary ocean liner while shooting *Aviator* and in a featured role as a lawyer in a courthouse scene for the movie *Hoover*. My only direction from the director, Clint Eastwood, was "look lawyerly."

As an extra, you are forbidden to speak to any of the main actors. Doing so is cause for immediate dismissal. Mingling with all those megastars was surreal. While filming the movie *Angels and Demons* for 16 days, I found out firsthand that Tom Hanks and the director Ron Howard are as nice as they seem. During the wee hours of the morning, they casually chatted and joked with us between takes. I got my union and Screen Actors Guild card in the middle of that shoot, which meant better pay and steak for dinner instead of pizza.

Did you know that often a portion of the audience on many TV shows are paid to be there? Most shows are free to the public, but when needed, they pay actors to fill the remaining seats. I was compensated me over 100 times to watch shows like Deal or No Deal, Judge Judy, Judge Roy Brown, Let's Make a Deal, the Bill Maher show, and many others. Compensation was only minimum wage, but it was a lot of fun.

I was in two reality shows, *Spying on Myself*, on the A&E Network, and *Master Chef 5*. On *Spying on Myself*, I would meet a former employee of mine who had stolen a client and caused me to lose over $100,000. The producers planned to lure her to a restaurant on the false premise of landing a job at my fictitious company. I would be in disguise and hopefully, she wouldn't recognize me. During the interview, I would ask her about her former boss (me) and have her tell me what she thought of him.

In order to pull of mu disguise, Brad Pitt's voice coach taught me a southern dialect. The make-up department created fake teeth and a wig. They even shaved off the hair on my arms and taught me to walk differently. When they finished my makeover, the disguise was so good I didn't even recognize myself.

My former employee arrived at the restaurant for her interview right on time. The whole restaurant was in on it, actors were at the tables, and there were hidden cameras at every angle. The plot was executed perfectly. I had a mic hidden in my left ear, and the director told me what to say. Finally, he had me take off my disguise, exposing the prank. The director came out from behind the hidden camera, and the actors began to laugh and clap. My ex-employee was totally shocked. She cried and apologized on national TV for what she had done to me. We hugged each other, and I forgave her.

Here's the secret you're not supposed to know. I wasn't able to locate my former employee, so the producers found an actress to play the part. No one except my agent and the producer knew about this. That's Hollywood for you. You never know what is real and what is fake. I will go with "mostly fake."

Over 5,000 auditioned for Master Chef 5, and I was one of the 100 contestants who made the final cut. The directors are masters at orchestrating drama and conflict between the contestants. As we arrived, they confiscated our phones and computers and locked us in a hotel room with another contestant. Luckily, they paired me with a great roommate. Believe it or not, his signature dish was cooking Python. If I needed to leave my room for any reason, I had to summon someone to unlock the door and escort me where I needed to go. They worked us so hard we only got 5 hours of sleep each night, so emotions became raw, arguments ensued, alliances formed, and gossip flowed. You can imagine the intensity, all in pursuit of the "prize." Towards the end, the producers became lax, and contestants were sneaking into other's rooms to have sex. People will be people.

I championed past 47 other cooks before Gordon Ramsey booted me off the show. He didn't like my choice of fresh cranberry sauce to cleanse the palette between a shrimp and pasta dish. At least I made it past the man who had a monkey as a sous chef and my roommate serving python.

When I got booted from Master Chef 5, they immediately put me in a room with a psychiatrist. The producers want to make sure that contestants don't "go postal" on them.

Why Hollywood?

So, why was I guided to move to LA and pursue a Hollywood career? It certainly wasn't for the money or stardom.

Remember the vision I had about the six women and the bride? Well, during the 12 years I spent in Hollywood, I met and fell in love with Carmela, and then Kerri, both were absolute angels. In the 13 years I've known Kerri, not once have I seen her be unkind. She taught me how to resolve issues lovingly. I wouldn't be where I am today without the love and kindness of both Kerri and Carmela. I didn't know it then, but they were teaching me what I needed to know to prepare me for meeting my bride, the final, serious relationship in this life.

Soul Recognition

"I recognized you instantly. All of our lives flashed through my mind in a split second. I felt a pull so strongly towards you that I almost couldn't stop it."
— *J. Sterling, In Dreams*

Have you experienced meeting someone and feeling like you already know them, where there's an instant connection? Chances are, they are probably in your soul group, a group you've incarnated with many times before. They're in your life again by prior agreement, to play a minor or significant role. Research shows that once a soul agrees to play a role in your life, they decide how, when, and where they will meet you. Sometimes though, even with all the planning, the souls do in Heaven, they miss connecting here on Earth. You would think this would be a perfect science, but it is not. More on Soul Groups later.

The second I set eyes on Kerri and Carmela, a vision of someone else flashed before me. Maybe it was their soul-self that I saw. Both times it shocked me so much that it is etched in my memory. With Connie, the same thing happened when she smiled at me as I entered the classroom at clown camp.

Chapter 21

I'm a Hypnotherapist

Because of the devastating financial crisis of 2008, my performing career had all but vanished. Companies slashed spending on entertainment, and I could no longer get my fee of $4,000 per show. The meager amounts I negotiated weren't enough to pay my bills. Now, what do I do? I couldn't count on movie roles to make up the difference.

Out of the blue, Kerri said, why don't we become Hypnotherapists? Kerri had seen an ad from a Hypnotherapy School offering a free two-week introductory course. Here we go again, we both enrolled. The Hypnosis Motivational Institute is the best known, fully accredited school for hypnosis in the US, and it was only a few miles away. I spent the next two years immersed in this fascinating field, excited about starting a new career.

My days as a comedian and actor slowly faded into the background over the next four years as my new career as a therapist emerged.

Home Free

I called my therapy practice, Mobile Mind Repair, and instead of people coming to me, I made house calls. Soon I was traveling all over Southern California, Northern California, and parts of Mexico. Since I was traveling all over and rarely home, I decided to try an experiment. I gave up my apartment and moved into my RV. For the next eight years, I became "home free," as I called it, having the adventure of a lifetime.

To my surprise, I quickly adjusted to living in my RV. Every day was a new adventure, meeting people and having experiences I would never have had in LA. After decades of being responsible for a family, the freedom from bills and obligations was exhilarating. Imagine not having a mortgage or utilities, internet, and trash bills.

I prayed I would go wherever needed regardless of where it would take me, and oh, what a ride! I was about to witness the underbelly of the real world, to see the hidden pain behind the smiling masks of our personas, to feel the sadness, disappointment, and anguish of the walking wounded. I empathized with their guilt, shame, fears, and feelings of hopelessness.

Chapter 22
Taking Off My Rose-Colored Glasses

The moment you accept what troubles you've been given, the door will open.
                                              Rumi

Warning!

If you have a hard time hearing about other people's excruciating pain and trauma, skip to the next chapter. It is not my intent to traumatize you.

For the rest of you, I want to show you how God opened my eyes to the suffering on Earth and how that prepared me to be a Life Between Lives facilitator.

I had gone from a life of comedy and laughter to the flip side, the place where pain and suffering reside. I could no longer hide from the cruelty of this world. I was witnessing the harsh reality behind the curtain, and it's not pretty. With my rose-colored glasses off, I began to see and experience the world as it really is.

Why so much suffering? What is God's plan? Why do bad things happen to good people? How does a loving God allow all this? Why am I being exposed to all this suffering? The time I spent in Heaven and the research I'm doing with clients have provided me with many insights and answers.

Time after time, I found myself in the right place at the right time to help troubled souls heal. Later, I would come to realize that the pain and sadness of my clients were also a part of me. As they heal, I become healed. There are no coincidences.

Watching the Unthinkable

A friend referred me to Doug. He was grieving the tragic loss of his wife, the only person whom he had ever loved. His grief had overtaken him and was having a hard time functioning.

Doug was raised by an abusive father who showed him no love or affection. He said his wife was the first person who ever loved and cared for him. On the night of his wife's death, they shared a romantic dinner at their special restaurant. He remembers everything had been perfect, and he'd never been happier. On the drive home, a car sped through a red light and crashed into them with such force that their car rolled over and over, leaving them hanging upside down in their seat belts. When he came to, his wife was gazing at him with love and desperation. In a whispering, tearful voice, she said over and over, "I love you." He tried to respond, but couldn't get a word out. The crash had crushed his sternum.

He tried to no avail to say, "I love you too!" He vividly remembers the feelings of fear and hopelessness, knowing there was nothing he could do. He hung suspended upside down and watched as she slowly bleed out. Just as the ambulance arrived, she closed her eyes and drifted away. The depth of his pain was palpable as he shared his anguish. "She never got to hear me tell her I loved her too."

Murder at KFC

When I had clients in LA, I took a familiar route cutting through a Kentucky Fried Chicken parking lot on my way to Kerri's. One night I saw an altar lit with candles next to a streetlight pole on the edge of the parking lot. Amongst the candles was a photo of a young Hispanic man whom I assumed died there recently, and someone had constructed a memorial altar in his memory.

On my next trip to LA, I noticed the altar was still there and new candles were lit. A few months after that, as I walked through the parking lot, I saw a young woman kneeling at the candle-lit altar. I didn't want to interrupt her ritual but heeded that inner nudge. I stooped down and quietly introduced myself and told her I was a therapist that did grief counseling, and if she ever needed help, I would be happy to give her a free session. She thanked me, and I went on my way.

When I returned to LA three months later, I parked in my usual spot. It was 2:30 A.M., and I was exhausted from the eight-hour drive. I knew I'd be crossing the parking lot in a few minutes and wondered if the altar would still be there. Surely, after so many months, she must have moved on in her grieving process.

I closed my eyes and asked God why I was drawn to give this young lady my card if nothing was to come of it. At that moment my phone rang, and you guessed it, it was her. I told her I had just been wondering if she would ever call. We both knew it was divine intervention. She accepted my offer of free counseling.

Alexandria was 21 years old and had a 3-year-old daughter. Last New Year's Eve almost a year ago, her husband stopped into KFC to buy dinner for the family, and as he was leaving, another young Hispanic man and a woman walked by. The two men exchanged glances, and the other man didn't like the way Alexandria's husband looked at him, so he pulled out a gun and shot him twice in the back.

Alexandria was at work when she got the call. She rushed to the site and saw her husband lying lifeless in a pool of blood. She screamed and pounded her bloodied fists on the concrete as they draped a clean white blanket over his body.

Alexandria responded well in our session. Her sadness and worry about her daughter growing up without her father have lessened. She is planning to have a Life Between Lives session with me soon and excited about talking to her husband in Heaven.

Torture

One of my first clients was a beautiful soul named Freda from Costa Mesa, California. I helped her get rid of a phobia that almost caused the death of her husband. She asked if I would help her brother, Diego, overcome his issue.

What a wonderful, kind man Diego was, very gentle with a warm smile. Now in his early 60s, he wanted treatment for trauma resulting from severe torture when he was 17.

During the civil war in Nicaragua, government troops raided his town and mistook him for a rebel. They arrested and tortured him for several weeks, hoping to get information from him about the rebels. They hoisted him up like a side of beef in a butcher's shop and prodded his body with electrical rods. Each day it got more invasive, intensifying the voltage until he would pass out. Diego was not a rebel and knew nothing, but the torture went on for days.

They gave him one last chance, talk or die. There was nothing he could do. He heard the commander give the order to kill him. He watched as they turned up the prods to full power. The pain was so great he went into shock. A second later, he found himself outside of his body in the presence of an Angel who told him not to worry; he would get through it. His next memory was waking up in the dirt alley behind the jail.

Amazingly, he forgave the young men who tortured him long ago. He understood the government forced them into the army, and they had no choice but to follow orders. He realized they were just as damaged as he was.

He told me something good had come out of his ordeal. The out-of-body experience with the Angel led him on a lifelong search for

God. He was forever grateful for that wake-up call, and I am thankful for the opportunity to help him heal from the emotional, psychological, and physical torture he endured.

Handwriting Analysis Booth

When I was in San Diego seeing clients, I often set up a booth on weekends at Sea Port Village on San Diego Bay. I offered handwriting analysis, a skill I learned at Hypnotherapy College.

Only feet from the ocean, it felt like a slice of Heaven. I loved every minute, even though some days I didn't make a dime. It didn't matter because I knew that something special and magical would happen every time I opened my booth.

It seemed to be a way-station for troubled souls from all over the world. I analyzed handwriting, and often when people realized that I was a therapist, they opened up about their personal issues. Many times I ended up doing free therapy sessions for them.

I'd start my day with a simple meditation and prayer, "OK, God, I'm here. Who are you sending me today? Someone always showed up. Major Mike and Dave are examples of some troubled souls who came to my booth.

Killing Hundreds

Major Mike was most kind but very troubled. He hadn't been to his apartment in weeks, choosing instead to sleep in the bushes in a nearby park. He gave away his car and drank from morning till night to numb the never-ending, traumatic thoughts running through his head.

He was a major in the Army and commander of an attack helicopter in Iraq and Afghanistan. He had fired on targets many times without regard for collateral damage and was sure he had killed over 200 people, including women and children.

He was shot down twice, both times being the only survivor and losing his entire crew. In the second crash, he was buried under rubble for hours before being rescued. He showed me a scar from a bullet wound he received in a hand-to-hand fight with an Iraqi soldier. He also lost an eye when his Humvee ran over an IED. The list goes on ….

A few years ago, on the day of his welcome home party, his wife and daughter died in an auto accident. His remaining daughter followed in his footsteps and joined the Army only to be shot in the head in Afghanistan just months before. Who wouldn't want to numb themselves with alcohol all day?

Volunteering at a school kept him alive and functioning. He was a virtuoso cellist and taught music to children once a week. His music and the children gave him purpose and a reason to live. I wanted to continue helping him, but he disappeared. No one knows what happened to him.

Today, He Would Kill Himself

Dave hung around my booth until I closed even though I analyzed his handwriting hours earlier. As I packed up, he asked for my help. He told me he had flown here from Illinois, bought a knife when he arrived and planned to cut his wrists and bleed out on the beach behind me. He then raised his shirt to show me the knife in his waistband.

He helped me carry my things to my car, and we drove to a nearby park where he told me his story. He had abandoned his three young children 15 years ago and felt like a total failure. He was too cowardly to face the hatred that his children must have for him. Recently losing his job and the guilt and shame had become too much to bear. He wanted to go home to see his children but decided he would kill himself instead.

For four hours, I used every skill I had to help him reframe the way he looked at his life. He responded very well, and I could see him calm down. We even laughed a bit. I bought him dinner at Jack in the Box and dropped him off at the airport to fly back to see his kids. He handed me his knife. I don't know where he is now, but I know I saved a life that day and realized God had sent him to me for help.

Left for Dead

My longest term ongoing client Kim, is an amazing human being. She is kind, honest, and considerate and goes out of her way to help others despite enduring a lifetime of horrific abuse.

She is currently involved in a high profile civil case suing the city of Bakersfield, California, for the abuse she suffered for over three years at the hands of a police officer. She was sexually assaulted more than 40 times in his office and even at her home in front of her 16 year-old disabled son. Resisting would have meant the death of her children and herself. A recent expose in the Guardian reported that the Bakersfield Police Department is the most deadly and corrupt in the United States. The Sherriff Department there has a history of their officers raping and sexually molesting women and then paying them off so they wouldn't bring charges; some were paid as little as $200. Finally, they got sued for a million dollars, but that hasn't stopped them.

In retaliation for the lawsuit, the Bakersfield police have continued to abuse and harass her and her children for three years. I'm hoping she will write a book about all the abuse she has suffered because of the "Good Ol Boys Club" that is alive and well the Bakersfield police department.

Kim's PTSD is so severe that she has to have a full-time caregiver to help her deal with constant nightmares and severe daytime anxiety. Even with the best of therapy, she will be dealing with this for the rest of her life. Mark Geragos, one of America's high profile lawyers, has taken her case to get justice.

Kim's abuse started when she was a small child. Her stepfather physically, emotionally, and sexually abused her for years. He's done everything from dragging her down the hall by her hair and throwing her in her room to empting a jar of spiders in her room and turning off her light. That night, too afraid to move, she woke up with a spider crawling in her mouth. You get the idea.

Twelve-year-old Kim and a friend were kidnapped at a mall and taken to the Arizona desert where they were sexually assaulted for days. This savage held cutting shears to their throats, forcing them to please him sexually. She learned that the only way to survive was to submit and befriend her captor. He let his guard down one day and drove them to town. At a traffic light, they jumped from his car and ran to safety.

While vacationing with her mother in Mexico when she was 16, a cab driver kidnapped her, took her to a remote area and raped her, he said he was going to have to kill her, but somehow she managed to befriend him too, and he let her go.

In her early twenties, she came home to find a stalker in her apartment who raped and tortured her for two days. At one point, he made her dye her hair to look like his girlfriend, who had just broken up with him. He said he couldn't kill his girlfriend but would kill her instead. Finally, he beat her unconscious and left her for dead, but she came to and crawled out of her apartment, desperate for help. Again, she survived.

All of this seems too much to bear for anyone's lifetime, but Kim's abuse continued. In her 30s, a Bakersfield police officer pulled her car over with her three kids in the car, handcuffed her, put her in the back of his patrol car, and drove around trying to find a hotel room so he could rape her. Luckily for her, they were no vacancies due to forest fires in the area.

Throughout her marriage, her husband regularly beat and berated her breaking her nose twice, causing her to have her nose reconstructed.

The Bakersfield police recently shot her 21-year-old son as he was driving an unreturned rental car for a friend. As a result, he is paralyzed from the neck down and awaiting trial. He is represented by another high profile lawyer that has vowed to get him justice.

You're probably asking, as I continually do, how could anyone survive this kind of torture and still be a loving, kind, and trusting person? Kim is the strongest and most remarkable person I have known. Due to the severity of her PTSD, progress has been slow, but she is determined to do all she can to heal.

Suicide by Hanging

Helen came home from work a few months ago to find her husband hanging from the rafters in their garage. All she could do was scream at the top of her lungs. She realized that his childhood trauma was more than he could endure.

She came to me for a Life Between Lives session, hoping to connect with him in Heaven, and she did. It was one of the most moving sessions I have had.

During my time in Heaven, I relived the moment when I decided to come to Earth to do this work. They advised me how emotionally hard it would be, and I could have backed out then, but I didn't. I love this work despite how emotionally taxing it is.

Chapter 23

Mexico Awaits Me

"It's only after you've stepped outside your comfort zone that you begin to change, grow, and transform." — Roy T. Bennett

Four years ago, **I could** not have predicted nor imagined the depths of intimacy, healing, and pain that I would witness and experience. I loved being "home free." In actuality, I spent very few nights in my RV. I lived on a boat for six months in a marina near Venice Beach, stayed with family when seeing clients in Sacramento, and a client offered a room in her home in Orange County anytime I had client sessions near her.

When I was in San Diego, I preferred sleeping in my RV. The magical place where I camped for the night was 40 feet from the bay. I loved waking up to the sounds of gentle lapping waves and squawking seagulls and found the fresh air and gentle sea breezes invigorating. It was the perfect place for me to rejuvenate and heal my mind, body, and soul from the intense work I was immersed in.

In February 2012, I got a call from my best friend, Tony, inviting me to visit him in Mexico. He said he knew a few Americans there who could benefit from my services. Why not, I thought, I vowed to go wherever I was needed. Besides, it would be an adventure.

Tony introduced me to his American friend Lamar who was suffering from severe PTSD from military service. He became my first client in Mexico. Lamar proposed a trade; I could live in his

beach house in exchange for therapy. I struck gold, I thought. We shook hands, and I moved in a few days later. I loved listening to the rhythmic ocean waves crashing against the seawalls 24/7. As it turned out, I lived in that beach house for a year and a half.

I came to realize Lamar wasn't ready to face his demons. We'd start a session, and 15 minutes into it, he'd say, "That's enough, I'm done." To my dismay, we only did two 15-minute sessions during the entire time I was there. As much as I wanted to help him, I learned that I couldn't coax anyone into therapy that isn't ready.

I wondered why my inner guidance led me to this cozy cottage 100 feet from the ocean. What were the lessons waiting for me? I had given up my anchors, no more acting or performing to rely on.

Living in Mexico was a huge learning experience for me. I was immersed in the culture and saw how families had joy and happiness without all the materialism and conveniences we enjoy in the US. I became friends with families that slept six people in the space of a 2-car garage. People worked 10 hours a day, making a meager $20 and somehow fed their families. During the time I lived there, I got nothing but smiles and kindness from everyone I met. I have so much love and respect for the Mexican people.

Mexico's Dark Side

Please know I'm not suggesting Mexico doesn't have a dark underbelly. It is a troubled and violent country with deep-rooted, pervasive corruption. I lived in Primo Tapia, and a store owner told me that every business in town was forced to pay protection money to the police monthly. Over 40,000 foreigners are living in Baja, mostly at the beach in the 90 miles between Tijuana and Ensenada. They carry extra cash in their wallets to pay bribes to the police who stop them for bogus reasons and demand payment on the spot. One man just shrugged his shoulders and said, "That's just the way it is, you get used to it, and it's no big deal."

The first person I met in Mexico was Richard, who met me as I crossed the border and guided me to my friend Tony. Richard was a retired contractor who moved from Bakersfield, California, to La Mission, a small coastal town 40 miles south of the border. His beautiful home, perched on a cliff 50 feet above the ocean, had a million-dollar view. He had spent over $80,000, remolding it into a swanky bachelor pad. His parrot named "Captain Jack" lived in a huge cage just outside his front door, and on weekends, he took Captain Jack into town and charged tourists $5 for a photo opp.

Richard came home one day to find his front door padlocked and all of his belongings in a pile in front of the house. The local police had evicted him, claiming that the house belonged to someone else. Unfortunately, the person who sold him the house was not the legal owner. Richard lost everything and was so distraught that he broke his eight years of sobriety. A few weeks later, he got into a bar fight and was stabbed to death. I don't know what happened to Captain Jack.

On my first day in Mexico, Richard and Tony drove me around town. Tony was drinking a beer and assured me it was no big deal as you could do whatever you wanted here. Minutes later, we got pulled over by the police. Because I was sitting in the back, Tony quickly handed me his beer as the police approached. They made us get out of the car to search it and found the open beer bottle where I was sitting, so they assumed it was mine. The policeman questioning me and got frustrated when it was obvious I didn't understand Spanish, so he made us follow him to the police station.

I had heard horror stories about the corrupt police in Mexico and was afraid of what they would do to me. The police chief, Captain Ventura, came out of the station and asked what was going on. Just as they were figuring out what to do with us, Jeremy, a friend of Tony's drove by. He stopped and spoke to the captain, and a few minutes later, we were released.

We found out later that Jeremy recently had done a favor for Captain Ventura, so he reciprocated. I was so relieved. My first hours in Mexico and already, I was wondering if I had made a mistake coming here. About six months later, I found out that Captain Ventura, his wife, and daughter were all murdered as they walked out of a soccer game. Captain Ventura had hassled the son of a cartel boss, and the cartel retaliated.

My friend Tony was kidnapped twice during the two years he lived there. Somehow he continually finds himself living on the edge and hanging out with the wrong people. Tony made a $10,000 deal to sell inflatable bounce houses to a guy who was opening a kid's playhouse in a mall 50 miles inland. Tony had a contact in China who manufactured them. When he delivered the product, the merchant held him at gunpoint and robbed him of everything. Tony was now powerless and penniless and couldn't even pay the translator he had hired. What Tony didn't know was that the translator was a low-level cartel member.

A few days later, the cartel kidnapped Tony and his girlfriend, taking them to their compound. Every day they threatened to kill them. Tony's ability to charm his captors saved them. He has a way about him, an infectious enthusiasm for life that draws people toward him. Their ordeal ended after two weeks when the compound gates opened, and they were set free. They were not unscathed; both suffer severe PTSD from the ordeal. I can only imagine the hopelessness and mental torture they endured believing every day was their last. A few months later, a rival cartel beheaded the men who kidnapped Tony and his girlfriend for an unrelated reason.

Lorena, Ex Cartel Boss

Tony befriended a woman named Lorena, an ex-cartel boss who had a reputation for beheading her rivals. She had been on the losing end of a war with another cartel, and finally got out of the business.

She found religion and is now a priestess in Santeria, a religion that is a mix of West African beliefs mixed in with Catholicism that came out of Cuba. I was surprised when I learned that it is one of the fastest-growing religions in the United States.

When Tony took me to meet Lorena, she wouldn't let me in her home until she confirmed I wasn't bringing in any evil spirits. She had me take off my shoes and then threw a half dozen seashells at my feet. They arranged themselves in the proper order, and she said, "Good energy." She gave me a tour of her home, showing me three different altars, each used for different purposes. That evening, we all drove to Thursday night Karaoke where she asked me to dance. What am I getting into, this would definitely be toxic. A few days later, Tony told me she had taken a liking to me wanted to see me again. Luckily, I was leaving for the states, and when I returned to Mexico, I diplomatically kept my distance.

Gang Revenge

I got to know Tito when he came to clean the beach house every week. I liked him. He had a great sense of humor, and we became friends. As we got to know each other, and he found out I was a therapist, he began to open up about his life.

Tito was deported from the US after spending 22 years in prison. His wife and child still live in the US, and he only sees them when they visit Mexico. I was curious why he spent so many years in prison and he shared his story.

Tito crossed illegally into the US with his parents when he was a child. As a teenager, he joined a gang in LA, married and had a daughter. One day while taking his wife and daughter to a doctor's appointment, his wife wanted to stop at Jack in the Box. He said no because it was in a rival gang's territory. She insisted as it was just off the freeway and on the way to the doctor's office.

As they pulled into the drive-thru, members of the rival gang spotted Tito. They surrounded the car, pulled out their weapons, and fired into the vehicle. Tito ducked down, shoved his foot on the accelerator, sending his car over the curbed drive-through lane and into oncoming traffic. Thirteen bullet holes in the car and miraculously, none hit him, his wife or daughter. Furious, he took his family home, grabbed his gun, and vowed to retaliate. Over the next two weeks, he went on a rampage, stalking and shooting 11 members of the rival gang, killing nine.

I had never been in the presence of a murderer. Tito didn't seem to be a bad person. He tried his best to explain his mindset and emotional state as he hunted down and killed all those men. Blinded with rage, it seemed as if another person was pulling the trigger. He has very little memory of the actual killings.

While in prison, he had an out-of-body experience that changed everything. He grew up, matured, and became a different person. Well, he hasn't totally changed. Once in a while, he borrows his friend's police uniform on weekends and writes fake tickets, forcing tourists to pay him on the spot. He claims it's the only way to survive.

An Evil Man

Brad was engaged to one of my clients. One night they got into a screaming match, and she stormed off in her car fleeing from his violent rage. He took everything she owned, dumped it in the driveway, poured gas all over it, and lit a match. All of her photos, all her clothes, the manuscript of the book she was writing, her new wedding gown, everything turned to ashes. Luckily, a few months later, she was able to extricate herself from him, though he continued to stalk her for months.

I worked with Brad for anger management issues but dropped him as a client because I felt he was dangerous. Some people are just evil. The last I heard, he was dating a transvestite and living in Tijuana. No, I'm not kidding.

American Fugitives

I once met an American at a Sunday Brunch, and he was already intoxicated. When I asked him how he came to live in Mexico, he said he had killed a man in a bar fight 12 years earlier, and fled to Mexico and is still afraid to go back. I discovered lots of fugitives live in Mexico.

Chapter 24
Clients in Mexico

It didn't seem to matter where I went, people would find me to help them heal. Here a few of my clients I met in Mexico.

The Debutant Coyote

Alisha is from one of America's wealthiest families. Her father sexually abused her for six years. Her parents shipped her off to Oxford University in England, and upon graduating, they expected her to return home to join the world of high society. Her resulting PTSD was too much, so she rebelled, left college, and fled to Mexico. When I met her, she was living in an abandoned home in a little town called La Mission, 45 miles south of the US border. She had no electricity, water or plumbing and had 13 dogs she had rescued. She had completely cut herself off from her family.

During one of our sessions, Alisha told me when she was seven years old, she saw her father going into her younger sister's bedroom in the middle of the night. She knew what that meant. Powerless to save her sister, she set the house on fire. At least for that day, her sister was safe. She said, by the time her mother was willing to face the harsh reality, her father had molested all three of his daughters for years. Her parents divorced.

Out of compassion for the impoverished Mexican people, it became her mission to smuggle people into the US. She took them by boat, sailing miles out into the ocean, and brought them back on the US side of the border near San Diego.

During Alisha's first trip, when she was in open water miles from the coast, she spotted what she thought was a seal bobbing on the sea. It was actually a man frantically treading water, trying to stay alive. After rescuing him, he told her that earlier in the day, he was on another crowded boat with others trying to get to America. The coyotes (smugglers) got word that the Coast Guard was on their tail, so they threw everyone overboard. He was the only one who survived.

A few months later, as Alisha docked in San Diego with another boat full of illegals, the border patrol caught her. After spending months in prison and gaining 70 pounds, she was released on parole. She immediately crossed back to Mexico, breaking her parole conditions.

She responded well to therapy and was able to heal from a lot of her abuse. She reentered the US and luckily didn't have to go back to prison to finish her sentence. She now lives in Florida with her mother.

Death by Chemo

When I arrived at Cathy's hotel in Tijuana, she greeted me with an amazing soulful, magnetic smile. She was a person who could light up any room and had an angelic quality, rare in today's world.

Battling breast cancer, Cathy was a high-level executive at Boeing and had been on sick leave for months. She tried traditional cancer treatments to no avail and was experimenting with alternative methods in Tijuana. She and her husband sold all they owned and were now over $200,000 in debt.

Cathy had done her due diligence and probably knew more about alternative cures than anyone on the planet. Her apartment was filled with all kinds of gadgets and potions to eradicate her cancer. The alternative treatment was working, and she showed me the photos that proved her tumors were almost gone. Her US insurance agreed to provide more funds for her alternative protocol on the condition that she come back to the states and go through one more round of chemo. Reluctantly, she agreed. She flew back to the US and went through the procedure, and it caused her cancer to metastasize. Now, cancer was rapidly spreading throughout her body.

Furious about the antiquated, barbaric, traditional treatment she was forced to endure, Cathy and was back in Tijuana resuming her alternative treatment. She was hoping hypnosis would stimulate her subconscious to accelerate her healing. The first two sessions went well, and she booked another for the next month.

When I called to confirm our session, I got no answer. A few days later, I tried again, and her daughter answered. She told me that, sadly, her mother died a few weeks ago.

I sat in my car and cried. My first client had died.

Shot in the Leg

Twenty-year-old Brandon told me his story. As the sun came up one morning a year ago, he opened his eyes to find himself next to a dumpster in a seedy area of Portland. His clothes were soaked from the light rain that had fallen throughout the night, and he felt excruciating pain in his left leg. Memories came back to him in fragments. He could feel the bullet in his bloodied leg. He wondered if the man he shot was dead. If so, the other gang members would surely come after him. It was supposed to be simple, like the other times. He gave them the drugs, and they gave him the money. "It just got crazy," he said. Until last night, selling drugs had been all fun and games.

As he laid in pain, Brandon thought, what if my mom knew what I've become? The thought of that sickened him. I can never let my mother find out I'm dealing drugs. That day was his "bottom." He vowed to get help and overcome his drug addiction and to never, ever, sell drugs again. He told his father, not his mother, about his drug addiction and asked for help. Brandon's supportive father moved him to their summer home in Mexico to get away from all the bad influences. Fearing a relapse, his father contacted me to help him stay straight.

Chapter 25
Becoming an Author

I **had always wanted to** write a book, but my excuse was I never had the time. While I sat on the patio overlooking the ocean in Mexico, it occurred to me that I had nothing but time, so I decided to write my biography.

Writing about my life became a spiritual experience. I put myself in a trance state and regressed myself to my earliest childhood memory and then moved forward in time journaling about every experience I could remember. It amazed me how much I had forgotten. The more I wrote, the more my life came into focus. I saw threads of a divine presence ushering me from one experience to another. My life, with all its twists and turns, began to make sense. So, where do I go from here? Am I at my final destination, or does God have other plans?

Booted out of Mexico

When I finished my biography, I was on a roll and couldn't stop writing. I wrote and published three other books on different therapy topics. The day after I finished my last book, Lamar, in a drunken stupor, banged on my door and said, "I think it is time for you to get the hell out." Surprisingly, the shock and impact of this only lasted a few minutes. I realized the timing was perfect since I just finished writing my 4th book a few hours ago. God was sending a clue that it was time to move on.

I switched into "glass half full mode." I didn't know where I would go, but every time I followed my inner guidance, things always worked out. My excitement was building as I cleaned every nook and cranny in the beach house, loaded my car, gave Lamar a big hug, and was cruising towards the border in less than four hours. A few days ago, I thought I would be in Mexico for years, but in an instant, I was booted out and headed towards a whole new chapter in my life. It amazed me how quickly my state of mind and mood shifted.

Chapter 26

Mom Needs Me

A **few weeks after leaving** Mexico, I got a call from my sister Anne letting me know that my 91-year-old mother could no longer care for herself and was moving in with her. I moved back to Sacramento and spent the next year being with family until my mother passed away. I was blessed to spend more quality time with her than I had in the prior 30 years.

About eight months later, it became too difficult for my Anne and her husband to care for my mom, so she moved into a care facility. She deteriorated rapidly, and within a few months, she was so weak she chose to go into Hospice.

My mom made a conscious choice to stop all food and medication. It was hard on all of us as we watched her starve herself to death over the next two weeks. In Oregon, she could have had an injection and ended it quickly, but in California, that is against the law. Starving yourself to death is the only legal option. Where is humanity in that?

The last vision I have of my mother was two days before she died. She opened her eyes and smiled beautifully at me. I felt so much love coming from her. Then she gently closed her eyes and drifted back into her mind. I took a moment to memorize what would be the last connection with her is this life. I have thought of that moment hundreds of times since.

In my experience in Heaven, my mother gave me the same soulful smile again.

Finally, the Bride

As I was browsing profiles on an online dating site, I was captivated by the profile of a woman with the most inviting and soulful eyes. When I read the Rumi quote she posted, I knew that I had to meet her.

On our first date, I had that magical soul recognition experience, just like I had with Kerri, Carmela, and Connie, but the feeling was more profound. When I glanced at Patti, the faces of three unknown women appeared. It caught me off guard, and it took me a moment to regain my composure. That is very interesting, I thought.

I was immediately comfortable around Patti, and we talked and laughed about anything and everything for hours. While there was always magic in the air, we dated as friends, not lovers, for a year. I became discouraged. Maybe this is all it's supposed to be, I thought.

A week later, I attended an Eckankar seminar in Monterey, CA. and during a spiritual exercise, I had a vision. I was standing on a dock, and a boat was sailing off with Kerri (my most recent significant other) and her boyfriend waving goodbye to me. I had peace of mind knowing that Kerri was content and in love again and knew it was ok for me to move on in my life. Startled by a noise behind me, I turned around just as Rebazar, an inner teacher of mine, was escorting a woman off another boat. She laughed lightheartedly as she tripped on her wedding dress. She was wearing a veil with blonde hair flowing from it.

Seeing that, pulled out of the trance. A wedding dress? What's this all about? Then I recalled the vision I had 12 years ago; six women and a bride and the words, "That is all for this lifetime." I then realized there had been six significant relationships in my life.

The next day, during another spiritual exercise called, "God Has a Gift for You," I saw a vision the moment I closed my eyes. I was rowing a boat up to Patti's home. (It's on a river that flows into the ocean.) As I approached, Patti came running out, smiling from ear to ear. She was so excited; she ran right into the river waist-deep. With an exuberant, angelic smile, she placed a box on the palm of her right hand and opened it. I gasped. It was a shiny wedding ring.

By the next month, our relationship shifted from friends to lovers and within two years to committed lifelong partners. All my primary relationships had been leading me to my bride. I am at peace.

Chapter 27

Death's Doorway

By 2016, I had been engrossed in the tragedies and despair of my clients for seven years, and it had taken its toll on me. My emotions were raw, where I was getting sick every couple of months. I now understood why therapists have a high suicide rate.

As you will read, on my trip to Heaven, my guide told me to do four things to keep me from taking on the energy of my clients. If I didn't do these four things, I could become sick and die.

In August 2016, something felt terribly wrong during the four days leading up to our trip to Hawaii, a birthday gift from Patti. I thought I was just getting over heatstroke from helping a friend paint his house in 100+ degree weather the week before. Like most men, I minimized the symptoms, thinking I had a bad cold and could tough it out. By the time we landed in Kauai, I was so ill we immediately went to the hospital.

After taking x-rays of my lungs, I overheard a nurse say I might have advanced lung cancer and was airlifted from Kauai to Honolulu in a hurry. (They billed me $25,000 for the 100-mile flight. Something is wrong with our health system.)

A week and a biopsy later, I was diagnosed not with cancer, but with Valley Fever, which can sometimes be fatal, especially for those over 60. I was close to death and spent 22 days in the hospital in Honolulu.

I surprised myself at how calm I was throughout this experience, feeling an inner peace most of the time. I never slipped into victim mode, and if it was my time to die, I was ok with it. They pumped over $90,000 of drugs into me, and I began to heal. Already thin, I lost 30 pounds and couldn't navigate getting out of bed without help. When they discharged me, I could barely walk to the cab to take me to the airport.

This may sound unbelievable to you, but I'm grateful for the experience. In my diary, I listed twenty positive aspects and only one negative which was the hospital food. I now have more empathy for people going through their health crisis and a higher capacity to feel the love of my family and friends. While in the hospital, my sister Anne sent me heartfelt cards every few days; my younger sister, Mary, asked permission for Mormon elders to visit. Two young men visited, and we talked for hours about God and life. I was happy to see them when they came back two more times.

The nurses and doctors were kind and compassionate. One of them, knowing I was craving watermelon, went to the store, bought one, cut it up, and brought it to me. She opened up, knowing I was a therapist, and we talked on and off during her shifts about her upcoming marriage.

Another nurse often visited me on his night shift in the middle of the night, and we would have long talks about God. He was a young, handsome Hawaiian, and surfing was his daily spiritual exercise. He told me how other surfers would tease him as they walked by and saw him meditating at the beach each morning at sunrise. One day as he was meditating, he opened his eyes, and these same young men were sitting next to him meditating right along with him — what a great story.

While in the hospital, I had a lot of time to think about my life and what might be next in my practice. Michael Newton's book, *Journey of Souls*, came to mind. I had read it 20 years ago and had completely forgotten about it. I explored the Newton Institute website, and I found out therapists were being trained and certified to carry on Michael's research into the afterlife. Instantly, I was certain my calling was to become a Life Between Lives therapist.

Recovery

Recovery was longer than I expected. I still walked like an old man, having trouble climbing stairs and keeping my balance, but each day I was improving. I have a loving family, and my brother and my sister-in-law invited me to recover at their home in Sacramento. I stayed there for several months recovering in a private apartment above their garage.

Being in a weakened state made me more vulnerable and authentic. Emotionally, it allowed me to develop my inner guidance and sense of self further, illuminating a clearer picture of me as soul. As I read more case histories of people who had had the Life Between Lives experience and explored the possibility of becoming trained by the Newton Institute, I felt more certain of my future.

Becoming a Composer

Facing death opens up all the senses. Here I am again, with nothing but time on my hands, just like in Mexico when I wrote four books. This time I decided to compose a song. I didn't know much about it, and was only somewhat proficient on the keyboard, but felt driven.

I began tinkering with the keys on my keyboard, and a miracle happened. My first song came easily to me, and that inspired another, and then another. Within two months, I composed 16 songs and produced a CD. My songs are now being played around the world, and I'm receiving royalty checks. Amazing things happen when I open myself up to a power greater than myself.

Chapter 28
A Fork in the Road

As I read case histories about Michael Newton's client's experiences in Heaven, I realized that all my life's experiences had been leading me to my ultimate mission. Everything now made sense. I couldn't have reached this point any other way. A fork in the road was ahead, and it was crystal clear which path to take.

My qualifications and experience matched most of the Newton Institute's strict requirements for acceptance into their certification program. However, I still needed advanced training in Past Life Regression to be admitted to their October program. Through a series of little miracles, I met the prerequisites and manifested the cost for the training in a nick of time.

Life Between Lives Training

Michael Newton started the institute ten years ago so that others would continue his research. In the last ten years, the institute has trained over 250 therapists from 40 different countries. He had fine-tuned the Life Between Lives process after facilitating over 7,000 life between lives sessions over the past 40 years. The goal of the Newton Institute is to train enough therapists around the world to make the LBL experience accessible for anyone.

The Training Begins

I couldn't help but notice that there was something special about the instructors. They emanated a certain glow and had a quiet yet powerful presence, giving them an angelic-like persona. Just being in their presence was inspiring. I want to be like them, I thought.

Twelve of us from all over the US, Canada, and Australia took part in the intensive certification training. The first day was overwhelming. The training manual was two inches thick and several hundred pages. On day five we would facilitate our first Life Between Lives session and also experience a session as a client. Now that excited me. How could I do this work if I hadn't experienced it myself?

By day three, I found my stride, and a deep bond was forming between all of us. Everyone there had a heart of gold and a desire to make a difference in the world.

On day four, we were asked to select a partner for role play and practice. I didn't know who to pick, so I waited until there was only one person left. Grant and I were paired. He was in his early 40s, from Australia and the kind of person everyone likes, charismatic, handsome, and funny. He has a huge heart and exudes compassion and kindness and was the perfect partner for me.

The LBL Process

Most people are successful in reaching the superconscious state needed to have the Life Between Lives experience because the Newton Institute has fine-tuned the process. Briefly, here is the process.

Since you have died many times before, going where you go in between your next life is familiar to you. For this to happen, you must achieve a certain depth of relaxation or trance state as we call it. There is no hurry as each client differs in the way they respond to the process. Some clients get there a few minutes, others in 30 to 60 minutes, but almost everyone gets there.

As a warmup exercise, the facilitator regresses you to earlier memories of your current life. The next step is one of the most memorable parts of the process. You regress to your mother's womb where you find yourself in full consciousness, about to be born.

The research shows that souls are in full consciousness while in the womb. They are fully aware that they are beginning another life and are preparing for their new adventure. It's not until they come out of the womb that God draws the curtain behind them, and they lose most of their memories as soul. The facilitator can sometimes procure information from the soul in the womb about why they chose this body, what their mission is, and what they hope to experience in their new life. Etc.

Exiting the womb, you pass through a tunnel and find yourself in a significant event in a past life. You explore that life going backward and forward on the timeline, reliving numerous events.

It's common for clients to see correlations between their past and current lives. They often recognize people in a past life as players in the life they are living now, providing them with a broader perspective of their current relationships.

You will witness your death in that past life. Then find yourself out of that body and in your spirit body ascending to the afterlife with the help of your guide. At this point, your Life Between Lives experience begins. In another chapter, I will outline the places we have discovered that you are likely to experience.

During your journey, you will see a cast of characters and get answers to the questions you've prepared. Your facilitator will let you lead the way and remain there exploring for as long as you like. You will know when it's time to return to your earthly body.

Facilitating a Past Life Regression

On day four, as a warmup for my first Life Between Lives session, I facilitated a past life regression using the Newton method for Grant.

I had done many past life regressions for clients in my practice, but this method is much more precise. The client goes to a much deeper level of trance.

I jumped right in; Grant is a recognized medium in Australia and has appeared on TV many times as such. He receives messages from souls in the afterlife and conveys them to his clients. I'm glad I knew this because it helped explain what happened next.

Grant moved into a trance so quickly it shocked me. I didn't even get to follow the guidelines. He jumped way ahead of me. He slid right into a past life and easily answered all that I asked as he moved up and down the timeline of that life. I was amazed by how easy it was for him to split his consciousness and revisit a past life. So far, in my practice only one person has moved to a past life as quickly as he did.

Grant Guides Me in a Past Life Session

I had experienced past lives before, but not through hypnosis. Hypnosis is more direct and you don't have to wait for a dream, vision, or miracle. You close your eyes, and the therapists guide you along the way to that past life. It's so safe and straightforward, yet I was anxious about not being able to get there.

It went well initially. I had no problem bringing forth vivid memories of my current life. It was pleasant to relive some of them.

At the point where I knew Grant would regress me into my mother's womb, I became so anxious that it caused me to lose the depth of my trance. He deepened me but, as hard as I tried, I couldn't experience being in my mother's womb. He brought me out of hypnosis, and we called it a day. I was disappointed. Why had I been afraid to experience being in my mother's womb? When everyone returned to the training room and shared their experience, I was the only one who got stuck and unable to have that experience.

That evening, a facilitator worked with me for a few hours to help me remove my mental block about having the womb experience. She is a great therapist and did EFT (Tapping) with me on issues that came up. At the end of our session, she asked Grant if he would give it another go with me. He was more than happy to do so.

EFT also referred to as Tapping, is a modality now used by therapists all over the world. This modality is highly effective in releasing excess emotional energy held in the body. I wrote a few books on the subject.

Experiencing the womb is not a requisite for visiting a past life, but it's a bonus for people who have the experience.

My Second Attempt

This time I went to a deep state quickly and breezed right through my childhood memories, and without hesitation, I found myself in my mother's womb. It was dark and silent, and I could feel myself moving around. I felt my mother's sadness and fear of having her second child. I cried out loud as I felt her emotions. Because of this experience, I feel closer to my mother than ever before. I have to say that this was one of the most profound experiences I have ever had.

From there, I went to a past life where I was an Indian, teaching my son to hunt. I recognized him as my recent girlfriend's son, whom I am very close to.

I came out of hypnosis, feeling light and grateful. I did it! Grant was happy that he had been successful with me and knew I would do just fine tomorrow when we did our Life Between Lives sessions for the first time.

Knowing how important it would be, I went right to my room, laid out my clean clothes for the morning, sat up in my comfortable bed, and meditated for almost three hours. Relaxed, I fell asleep.

Facilitating My First Life Between Lives Session

I woke up anxious but optimistic. After breakfast, I would be the facilitator for Grant's LBL session. After lunch, it would be his turn to facilitate my LBL session.

All of my crazy life experiences brought me to this moment. The training had been intensive, technical, and detailed. Still, I worried, what if I lose my place and become lost? I met Grant in the session room. Kind, as usual, he reassured me again I would do just fine, and that calmed me down. Whatever happens, happens, he said. I closed my eyes for a moment and asked for guidance from the other side to help me through this.

He again moved quickly into a trance, through his childhood memories, into his mother's womb and seamlessly to a past life. He was a young girl named Gretchen, lugging buckets of water back and forth from town to her horses. I said, take me to your horses, and she replied, I can't. That was strange, I thought. Why not? She said because I have to cross this road and the oncoming wagon will run over me.

I'm stuck. Here he is in trance, in the body of a young girl realizing that a wagon will run over and kill her if she crosses the road. What a dilemma, I can't tell her to cross the road. I will not send her to her death. Then Grant's higher self speaks and says, "Tell her to cross the road. She needs to have this experience." I hesitated for a moment, then commanded, "Cross the road." A moment later, I ask, what is happening now? She said, "The wagon ran over me." I suggested she leave her body and watch from above the scene, and she said, no, I want to experience myself dying.

I waited a few minutes and then she said, ok, I'm out of my body now. Then I asked if she was ready to go home, where she goes in between lives? Gretchen said, not yet. I want to console the wagon driver. He's hysterical for having run over me. A minute later, she was ready to go to Heaven. As I began to speak, she interrupted me and said, I'm with my guide Merlin now, so you can skip ahead in the manual. At one point, she said, Regan, my guide Merlin wants to talk to you. I felt the hair on my arms stand up. Merlin said, "Regan, take a breath and calm down." We all laughed. A moment later, Grant merged with his higher self, the part of him that had remained in Heaven, and he joined the conversation. He told me the name he's called in Heaven. He couldn't pronounce it, so he sounded it out. It sounded like a mantra.

How bizarre to be having a conversation with Grant in the present day, Gretchen in another century, Grant's higher self and Merlin in Heaven, simultaneously. I was thrilled but confused. We found out that Grant was an evolved soul and had come down to Earth on a special mission to help raise the consciousness of others. He discovered a lot more but preferred to keep that private.

So, my first time facilitating was a great success. After lunch, it would be my turn to visit Heaven. I was about to have a life-changing experience.

Chapter 29
The Truth About Hypnosis

Some of you reading this may not have experienced hypnosis. Because there are so many misconceptions about hypnosis, I believe a little education is in order.

Frequently Asked Questions

Question: Will I be asleep during hypnosis?

Answer: The biggest misconception about hypnosis is that you go to sleep; you don't. You are awake and understand everything the hypnotist says. When you're in hypnosis, your body becomes very relaxed, yet your mind is very alert. It's similar to how you feel just before falling asleep or awakening in the morning.

Question: Can the hypnotist take over my mind and control me?

Answer: No, you are awake and in control at all times.

Question: What if I want to stop the session?

Answer: Easy, you tell the therapist you want to stop and just open your eyes.

Question: Can anyone be hypnotized?

Answer: Yes, as long as the person is willing to go along with the process. Some people are overly analytical and have a hard time relaxing, which can prevent them from being hypnotized. You can overcome that with practice.

Question: What is it like to be hypnotized?

Answer: Hypnosis is a natural state we experience on and off throughout the day. The therapist simply assists you in getting into that state. Daydreaming is a state of hypnosis. Meditation is self-hypnosis. Anytime you become singularly focused on one thing and shut out the rest of the world, you are in hypnosis, like when you are engrossed in a book or a movie.

Because hypnosis is a natural state of mind, most people have a successful Life Between Lives experience. The LBL facilitator will relax you to the edge of the awake and asleep state and keep you there. That is where the magic happens, where you have access to your subconscious and superconscious and memories of past lives and your time in Heaven.

Chapter 30
3 Hours 33 Minutes in Heaven – My Turn

I **prepared a list of questions** I wanted answers to when I'd be before the Council of Elders and a list of people I'd like to talk to in my Soul Group. How am I going to get my overthinking, analytical mind out of the way? All week, my instructors kept reminding me, "Out of your head and into your heart, Regan."

I skipped lunch and took a walk up the mountain behind the monastery. I was the only one on the trail and prayed that God would help me move into my heart during my session. I decided to use a technique that I've used successfully with my clients. I mocked up an image of my analytical self. He looked a bit "nerdy" with his white button-down shirt and pocket protector full of pens. We had a face-to-face, and he acknowledged his exhaustion from all that was going on. I suggested he take a break. "Let it go," I coaxed my analytical self as he walked down a long hall and went into the break room at the very end. I watched as he laid back in a comfortable chair and saw his tired and overworked mind began to relax. As I walked off the mountain, I knew I had done all that I could do to prepare myself. I got back to the center just in time for a light lunch.

My Life Between Lives Session Begins

Grant met me in the session room and again calmed me with his humor. I was comfortable with him knowing this was the first time he was facilitating an LBL session and I assured him not to worry, that he would do great. I closed my eyes. Grant asked me to take some slow, deep breaths, paying attention to the process of breathing. He had me hold my breath in the quiet place at the bottom of each breath, staying there longer before each successive breath. I began to relax.

Then, I imagined a golden liquid light slowly enveloping my body, relaxing every cell as it moved from my head to my toes. My body became motionless as I sank into the comfort of the cushions below me.

Grant guided me to a beautiful tropical island. With all of my senses activated, I walked in the warm surf, heard birds singing as they flew by, felt the grainy, soft sand between my toes and the warm rays of the sun drying my wet body.

At his suggestion, I floated up into the sky, miles, and miles above the Earth. He had me imagine a golden stairway with 67 steps, one step for every year of my life. Standing atop the stairway, I descended the steps, getting more and more relaxed and going deeper and deeper into trance. He stopped me on step 19 and I recalled memories at that age. Amazingly, I was flooded with images I had long since forgotten. Then he stopped me at step 13 and step 7, and more memories rushed back. He told me that this was a warmup exercise for when I get to my past life.

He then asked me to tell him about my earliest childhood memory. From there, I found myself getting younger and younger and smaller and smaller, and when Grant counted to three, BOOM, I found myself in my mother's womb again.

I'm writing about my experience in the session mostly in dialogue form, as it will be easier for you to follow. I've added commentary in italics so as not to confuse you. The commentary is necessary because when I had this experience, my consciousness was split. One part of me was in Heaven, the other fully aware and on Earth. The commentary in italics are the observations I was having watching the other part of myself in Heaven. It's one of the most amazing phenomena of this process, like watching a split-screen TV.

Grant: You are about to be born. Can you feel your body?

Regan: No, but I'm here in the womb. I can feel my mother's feelings.

Grant: When did you enter the fetus?

Regan: I don't know.

Grant: How is the brain in this body?

Regan: (laughing) Overloaded, I believe this life will stretch my physical brain to its limits.

Grant: What do you think about this life you are about to live?

Regan: It will be a doozy! I'm lucky in that there won't be problems like before, such as being shot, killed, drowned, run over by things, and murdered, and all that crazy stuff. This time it will be more emotional because I will feel the pain of people that have been going through what I went through in those other lives.

I cried, feeling my mother's emotions.

He now counted from 1 to 5, having me gently leave my mother's womb and float back up into space. As I viewed Earth from space, I felt happy and free.

At this point, I'm happy that things are going well, but know the next step is to visit a past life. Just thinking about it lessened my trance level, so I asked Grant to deepen me more. It took about 5 minutes before I was as deep as before. Next, I'm supposed to go through a tunnel and come out the end into another life. Instead, I went right into a past life.

As the scene unfolded, I began to cry again. I mean, really weep. I did not like what I was doing in that life and wasn't prepared for the emotions erupting in me.

Grant: What's going on?

Regan: I'm already here.

Grant: Tell me what's happening.

Regan: I'm a Roman soldier riding a white horse, and I'm in charge of what's going on.

Grant: What is your name?

Regan: Celius.

Grant: Tell me what you are seeing.

Regan/Celius: I see two rows of 4 or 5 men hanging from crosses, maybe more. There may be more, but that's all I see. I'm justified in killing them. These people are crazy. They believe in a man who says he is God and walked on water and raised a man from the dead. They deserve what I am giving them.

As the soldier, I feel justified in putting these Christians on the cross, but my Earth self, Regan, is tormented and crying like a baby. I'm feeling shame, guilt, and deep sadness for what I had done. How could I have brutalized so many? My higher self seemed to soothe me saying, Regan, you are not that person now. You have moved on. We are all bad before we're good. I can't handle the intense emotion, and I yell:

Regan: I'm sorry! I'm sorry! I'm sorry! Why did I do this?

Because of the intensity of my feelings as Regan, Grant suggests that I leave the body of Celius and look at the scene as if it was on a movie screen. In an instant, I found myself above the scene instead of in it, and my emotions began to subside.

For several minutes Grant had me take deep breaths to calm down. I've never cried like that or felt such sorrow, grief, or shame.

This process amazed me. I was here as Regan and in my past life as Celius and feeling the emotions of both of us at once. Hovering above it all, a third, higher part of me observed it all from a spiritual perspective. It looks like there are three of me now.

Grant: I want you to take me to an important scene later in your life as Celius. One, two, three, you are there. Tell me what's happening.

Regan/Celius: I'm with my grown daughter; she is all I have. I think I'm in my 70s and she is in her 30s. We are happy and content. "Fuck Caesar." *(I realize what I did in his name was wrong.)*

Grant: Take me now to the last moments of your life.

Regan/Celius: I'm lying on a table with my daughter by my side comforting me. I'm at peace, grateful I'm not dying by the sword. (A minute later) Now, I'm dead and above my body.

Grant: What was the biggest lesson you learned from your life as Celius?

Regan/Celius: Never to let anyone control me to do what I know is wrong.

As Regan, I know that the next step is going to where I go in-between lives, and I'm anxious. My trance depth was lessening, so I asked Grant to deepen me more, and off I went, floating up higher, and higher, above the Earth. Will I meet my Guide or Master? Who will it be?

Grant: What is going on around you now?

Regan: I'm just floating; it is very peaceful up here.

I seemed stuck in this dark, peaceful place; nothing was happening. Again, I had him deepen me.

Grant: What is happening now? What do you see or sense?

Regan: I sense Rebazar is near. I sense him more than see him. I can't look directly at him. He is transparent and out of focus.

Rebazar is a master I know from Eckankar. He has appeared many times in my dreams and contemplations. He is usually the one I see when I get a higher initiation on the inner planes. I'm more comfortable with him than any other Eck Masters.

Grant: What is your soul name?

I tried for the longest time to let the name come to me, but it didn't. Then an Eck word Shanti came to mind.

Regan: My name is Shanti.

It disappointed me that the name didn't come to me in a way that was more miraculous, like a voice or dramatic vision. Later, I found out that Shanti means "peace." That's the perfect name for me. I love it.

Regan: I'm seeing people I know in this life flashing quickly past me. I think you need to deepen me again.

He deepens more, but I'm still stuck. I'm concerned that I will not make it to Heaven, but Grant didn't give up on me. He continued to deepen me. Then suddenly.....

Regan: I see a reddish light off to my left. (I'm silent for a few minutes.)

Grant: Are you still seeing the reddish light?

Regan: My head is vibrating like I'm on a launching pad ready to take off, but I can't. I'm frustrated. My head is expanding. I'm stuck.

Shanti took over and began talking through me. It's as if the higher part of me merged with my Earthy self.

Shanti: Regan is holding me back, keeping me from letting go.

Grant: Regan, you need to experience this as Shanti.

I hear my higher self say, "Go away, Regan."

Shanti/Regan: I'm seeing more light now. Something is happening. (A moment later), I'm on a cliff, Wow! This is the same cliff I was standing on in a dream I had over 40 years ago. I was in a plane crash and survived. When I left the plane, I felt an evil presence and ran up a mountain trail to escape it. This evil presence chased me to the top of the mountain. I knew it would kill me. It cornered me at the edge of the cliff, the same cliff where I am now. I had to make a split-second decision: jump to safety into this giant hand coming up through the clouds or turn around and face whatever was chasing me.

Grant: What is happening now?

Getting more emotional

Shanti/Regan: Here I am full circle, back on top of the mountain.

Sarcastically to myself

I think I'm this hotshot, spiritually evolved person, yet I'm a phony because I never really faced the horrible fear that has been chasing me all my life. I can feel this monster behind me, and I don't know what it is.

Regan/ Shanti's voice rises in frustration and emotional torment.

Shanti/Regan: I'll never find out what this is! I'm feeling so stuck! The giant hand is coming up through the clouds again.

Grant: How would it feel to jump into the hand to safety?

Shanti/Regan: I was just thinking that.

Grant: Jump in the hand now.

Shanti: Ok.

Grant: On the count of three. One, two…

Shanti/Regan: Wait, I want to stand here for a minute.

Grant: When you're ready.

Shanti/Regan: I want to feel this fear for a moment. I don't want to run away. (Crying and breathing deeply)….. I'm going to turn around and face it!!!

I bravely turn around to face whatever it is.

Sadness from the depths of my soul erupts. Standing in front of me was not a big monster, but a single line of people that stretched down the mountain as far as I could see, hundreds of men, women, and children. I shouted to them, I'm sorry, please forgive me! I'm sorry! I'm sorry! I'm sorry! I could hardly breathe and was hyperventilating. Hearing me shouting, Grant broke in.

Grant: Tell me what's going on.

Shanti/Regan: (Weeping) There is a line of people all the way down the mountain waiting in line to forgive me for what I have done to them in all my previous lives, I'm staying here.

Grant: When you're done, tell me.

Grant waited in silence while I experienced what was going on with me in Heaven. After some time had passed, I spoke up.

Shanti/Regan: I'm done.

Grant: Tell me what happened so we can record this.

Shanti/Regan: The first person was an older man. He kissed me on the cheek and hugged me, saying, "I forgive you." Then the next person did the same. Person after person after person hugged and forgave me. The last was a little girl, about seven or eight. She had straight, long brown hair and the most beautiful smile. The sorrow I felt at this moment was so deep, so painful. "What did I do to you?" "I'm so sorry!" She gave me this angelic smile, her loving eyes penetrated mine to the depths of my being, and she gave me the warmest hug.

I find it hard to adequately explain the enormity of what occurred to me on the edge of that cliff. Having what felt like hundreds of people hug and forgive me for what I had done to them lifted mountains of guilt, shame, and sadness from my soul. I now understood the power of forgiveness. At that moment, I felt my essence expand throughout all of creation.

Grant: Is the giant hand still there?

Regan: Yes.

Grant: Jump into it.

I jumped into it. A moment later, I'm in space looking down at the Earth.

Grant: Why did you incarnate on Earth?

Shanti/Regan: To be a conduit for people's pain and to help them heal. To learn to let their pain filter through me into the universe. But I still need to learn how to do that in the physical form. Otherwise, I will get sick and possibly die, which almost happened last year.

Grant: Ask Rebazar how to release the pain and suffering that you absorb from others so you can live a healthy life.

Shanti/Regan: He says that I should do a spiritual exercise every day. Start with five minutes a day, then work up to 15 minutes. I should spend more time in nature. He also said do simple acts of kindness every day, even if that is only picking up someone's trash. Be sure and smile at people more. Last, connect with other therapists and ask them how they ground themselves. Oh, wow! He says when I get the hang of it, this negative energy will turn into love.

I'm being shown a giant hourglass. As I take on people's pain, it's filling up with sand and getting stuck in the middle, not allowing the sand to empty into the glass below. Rebazar says to keep it from getting clogged; I must do the things he mentioned. I'm seeing myself smiling at people, doing kind deeds, practicing my spiritual exercises, being in nature, and being more present with the people in my life. As I see myself doing all these things, the sand is emptying into the bottom part of the hourglass. Now I've let go of all the pain and negative energy.

Grant: Are there any other purposes for Regan's life?

Shanti/Regan: I'm to love all who show up in my life. I know why Patti and Kerri and Connie have shown up in my life. They are helping me grow and evolve. Rebazar says I am also a catalyst for their growth and development. I'm supposed to step-it up be a better grandfather, too. They are important to children's growth and development.

Grant: How does that feel?

Shanti/Regan: I love it. I commit now to being more present in my grandchildren's lives.

(Laughing) Even if that means playing Candyland with them over and over again. I love being around their energy. Spending time with them balances and heals me.

Grant: What else are you hoping to accomplish in your life?

Shanti/Regan: I must learn to be kind. Kind at any cost.

Grant: How many lives have I lived before?

Shanti/Regan: 576. It's been a slow but steady progression of spiritual unfolding. Rebazar is smiling at me and saying, "Slow because you are thick sometimes." (I laugh) He says breathe and relax because when I tighten, I cut off the flow. He's telling me again to do my spiritual exercises, meditation, walk in nature, and all the things will keep me in a calm state.

Grant: Ask Rebazar which life Regan received the most wisdom?

Rebazar/Regan: (Rebazar answering through Regan)

This one. Regan is getting avalanches of wisdom, but he is missing a lot. He needs to be even more open and take better care of his health because he won't be able to complete his mission with a sick body. He needs to be more mindful. If Regan is experiencing challenges, he needs to know he can come here for help. We learn wisdom a bit at a time, not all at once.

Shanti/Regan: I see an analogy in my mind about wisdom. A professor is writing an equation on the blackboard, searching for years and years to find the answer and then one day, Boom! Like a bomb going off, he solves it. Wisdom results from having life experiences, contemplation, and "letting go."

Grant: Ask Rebazar why you were shown your past life as Celius.

Shanti/Regan: He says it was for the contrast to show me who I once was, compared to who I am now, and to love and accept myself despite the sins of my past lives. Also, to understand how soul progresses from selfish to selfless, like Saint Paul, who persecuted Christians and then had an awakening.

Grant: Let's ask Rebazar now if we can move on. Ask him if there is a place of higher wisdom to go to.

Shanti/Regan: (moments of silence) Yes, he says. He is taking me to a Temple of Golden Wisdom. I'm there now, it's so expansive here, and everything is so clean. Rebazar says people often come here in the dream state.

Grant: Have you been here before?

Shanti/Regan: Rebazar says yes, that I have been here many times.

Grant: Ask Rebazar what happens next here.

Shanti/Regan: He is walking me down a hall. We are entering a room, and there are others here. It's a classroom, and a teacher is writing on the board. He wants me to know I can come here whenever I need an understanding of what to do with clients and other situations that come up in my life. (Smiling at me) He says that I'm gaining wisdom a bit at a time and need to keep my ego in check.

Grant: Can you tell me, Shanti, where the Council of Elders is?

Shanti/Regan: I'm there now.

It's interesting how immediate movement is in Heaven. You have a thought, and it manifests instantly.

I see a semicircle of five judges. I can only identify one of them, Lai Tsi. The others are wearing robes with hoods, and I can't see their faces.

Lai Tsi came to me once when I was in deep meditation about 20 years ago. He brought me here to this temple or another one like it. He led me to a banquet room with a huge table filled with the most delicious foods I had ever seen. I remember the colors were so vibrant. I ran to the table and began piling heaps of every kind of food on my plate, higher and higher. I looked up for a second and stopped in my tracks. Behind the table were bleachers filled with about a dozen spiritual masters. They were standing there smiling at me, the raised eyebrow kind of smile. In an instant, I understood the lesson. I felt ashamed and bowed my head for a moment. This food was for everyone, not just me. I was being selfish and not being considerate of others.

I came out of the vision and shook my head, still embarrassed how selfish I had been. What a lesson that was. They were, in the most loving way, bringing my attention to my selfishness. That experience has kept me from being selfish hundreds of times. I'm still working on it. Lai Tsi is smiling at me. He said he's proud of me for becoming a less selfish human.

Grant: How does that feel?

Shanti/Regan: It feels good. I like that I am becoming more selfless. Li Tsi is telling me there is no end to selflessness; there is always one more level. He's asking me to envision myself in a joyous state, climbing the stairs to selflessness.

Grant: Do you see any other elders now?

Shanti/Regan: Yes, I see another master but don't know his name. He came to me in a vision and told me he and the others have worked with me over many lifetimes. He said it is best to solve my problems by myself first because that way, I learn and evolve. If, after I have done my due diligence, I still need help, ask them to step in. He said always be respectful of another's time.

Grant: Is there another Elder that wants to talk to you?

Shanti/Regan: Now, another elder is communicating with me, a woman. I don't recall her working with me before, but I have seen her picture. She is Kata Daki. What a loving smile. She's telling me how proud she is of me for working so hard to develop the feminine side of myself. I'm smiling too. She said that was something that I was lacking. For many lifetimes, I have negated the importance of feminine energy. She says I'm doing a great job of balancing it out.

Grant: What do they say about your life as Celius.

Shanti/Regan: Don't beat myself up over it, because it was a lesson I chose to learn. Caesar controlled Celius and commanded him to do unspeakable things. Celius wasn't spiritually evolved enough in that life to refuse Caesars's orders. Maybe that's why Regan has trouble with authority figures and doesn't want to be under anyone's thumb.

We need rules and authority figures to keep us all from destroying each other, but Regan needs to learn discernment. Sometimes submitting to authority is the right thing to do.

Grant: Can you ask them other questions about your life as Regan?

Shanti/Regan: Yes.

Grant: Ask them if you should see clients as you have been, driving long distances to them, or is it better to have an office and be in one place.

Shanti/Regan: They say both for now because people in outlying areas need my help. Pursuing my idea of having a new therapy van would work well for that.

Grant: Next question, should you continue to be a comedian, or are those days a thing of the past?

Shanti/Regan: They say that I should always have humor in my life. Incorporating it into my talks and presentations on my LBL experience would be great. One reason I incarnated on Earth was to develop a sense of humor because I was acting too serious in recent past lives. I needed to learn to laugh at myself. A good sense of humor would help me stay in balance and maintain a childlike innocence.

Grant: Ok, next question. How does music fit into Regan's life?

Shanti/Regan: Music helps people transcend their physical selves.

Grant: What is the significance of Patti in your life?

Shanti/Regan: She is a strong woman and teaches me patience, kindness, and communication. I've had visions that it's our destiny to be together.

Grant: Ask the council if Shanti has lived on other planets or in other dimensions besides Earth.

Shanti/Regan: Sure, but I incarnate mostly on Earth.

Grant: Here is another question. What role is your best friend, Tony playing in your life?

Shanti/Regan: (laughing) Tony mirrors some of Regan's dysfunctions, his wild and adventurous side. I've always sensed that Tony and I were brothers or close friends in another life. I have sensed that we were con men in another life, going from village to village bilking people through our schemes.

Grant: What other information would the council like to impart to you.

Shanti/Regan: (I laugh) They're walking out. I guess I'm done here.

Grant: Where do you need to go next? What about going to your soul group?

Shanti/Regan: (A minute of silence) I'm walking into what seems to be a convention center. I'm with my soul group.

Grant: How many people in your soul group?

Shanti/Regan: Quite a few actually, 16 or 23?

Grant: Do you recognize anyone from your life as Regan?

Shanti/Regan: (30 seconds go by) Kerri's energy is here…….. I feel a Patti energy, like a smile. (More silence) And there's Regan's mom standing a distance away and smiling at me, but I don't see his father… or his brother, who passed away at age 21 from Muscular Dystrophy. (Long silence). I feel too much of Regan is here and not enough of me. It's causing things to be blurry.

Grant: (He deepens me more) Shanti wants you to go off to the side so I can talk to him easier.

It was a strange feeling hearing my higher self tell me to step aside for a minute. Now I'm deep in trance again and seeing and assimilating things through Shanti's eyes.

Shanti/Regan: I see his father and brother now and Regan's ex-wife Connie. She is soft and sweet. I see Patti and Kerri again. Kerri is lost, but she will figure things out. I see my sister Anne. She was my wife in another lifetime. I see shadows. They are colors, light forms. (Long silence) I'm stuck again.

Grant: Maybe it is time to move on.

 Shanti/Regan: Yes.

At this point, Grant asked me several questions for which I had no answers. I didn't see anything nor hear answers from my guide. Finally, Grant posed another question.

Grant: Is there somewhere else you would like to go?

Music came to mind, and instantly I found myself in the Music Room at the temple.

Shanti/Regan: I hear a violin. Rebazar is laying down the violin and says that Regan should sit still and listen to the music. He says that when Regan wants to compose music, he should remember this place and come here in his mind. He should sit in this chair, be still, and listen to what comes through. Rebazar added, "Say the word fish," and that anchor will lead you here. He is showing me notes on some fish hooks.

Grant: So, where else do you want to go?

Shanti/Regan: Rebazar is saying that I should practice coming to

Heaven so I can see him more often. He says the goal is to live in the world with one foot here in Heaven and one foot on Earth. That way,

I can access higher wisdom; to do that takes work, selflessness, and conviction. He says I'm progressing, but to keep up the work.

Grant: Is there anything else you need to do before we end this session?

Shanti/Regan: No, I think I'm done. Rebazar says we have more work to do, and he is looking forward to working with me again. It will be easier for me next time because I know the way. Rebazar says it was nice to meet you, Grant.

Grant: Nice to meet you too. Let's now thank everyone, your soul group, the council, Rebazar.

Shanti/Regan: I'll give him a hug. (Hugging Rebazar) Geez, he's strong.

Grant: How do you feel about what you've learned?

Shanti's final words

Shanti: Wow, there is always more to learn. Look, I'm always here, and Regan knows that. As I'm saying this, I know that Regan is aware too. It's kind of cool how this all works.

At this point, Grant gives me post-hypnotic suggestions that I integrate all I learned today into my life. He counts from 1 to 10 and brings me out of trance.

Regan: I'm back.

Grant: How do you feel?

Regan: Amazing! Being in two places at the same time was surreal. I knew that I was in Heaven, and another part of me was certain I was on the couch in this room with you.

Grant: You got stuck in a few places, but I'm glad we persisted, and you broke through to the other side.

Regan: You did a great job, Grant. Thank you so much. I'm lucky to have you as my partner.

Chapter 31

Debriefing

On the last day of class, everyone shared their experience in the afterlife. One by one, I listened to their stories. Our experiences were similar yet unique. All of us went before the council of elders and visited our soul groups, although the settings were different. It seems the Elders tailor the setting to each person. Some visited places I didn't, like the library and place of recreation.

My experience in Heaven differed from what I had imagined. Physics is different there, and I had to adjust to that. My mind had to interpret all that and sort it out in a way that I could grasp.

We all agreed that the world would change for the better if more people had this experience. People would stop playing the victim and realize that life's challenges are not curses but opportunities for growth.

If you take the journey, remember that in Heaven, matter is less dense than here. Energy changes form at will. If you want to go somewhere, instantly you are there. No need to talk, communication is telepathic. Your human brain and mind will have to filter everything you experience, sometimes with no frame of reference. It is an "out of this world" experience.

The effects of an LBL session last far beyond the session itself. Not a day goes by that I don't think about my time in Heaven. I learn more about myself every time I listen to the recording of my session. To my amazement, I'm still processing the experience two years later.

I love the fact that this isn't a once-in-a-lifetime event and I can visit Heaven as often as I want. It's been two years now, and I plan to go back in the near future. I am compiling a new list of questions and want to have more conversations with my mother, father, and brother, whom are already there.

Twelve Highlights of My LBL Session

The 3 hours and 33 minutes I spent in this process has completely changed my life. This is what I learned from my experience.

1. Heaven is real, and I am not alone. I have a rooting section and met some of them there.

2. Looking down at the Earth with a guide by my side and experiencing the moment when I enthusiastically committed to my life's mission has dramatically impacted my life. I know with certainty that my mission is to be Life Between Lives therapist and help others deal with their life's traumas.

3. I was warned that being around all of my clients' emotional pain from their current and past lives could kill me and was given four guidelines to keep that from happening.

4. What impacted me the most was standing at the edge of the cliff and being embraced and forgiven by scores of people who I had harmed in previous lives. A mountain of guilt, shame, and self-hatred was lifted from my soul. I have begun to love and accept myself genuinely. What an amazing gift that is.

5. I also learned that my life's mission included three other goals: develop a sense of humor, nurture the feminine side of myself and to be kind at all costs. Looking at my life, I can see that I have done well in those three areas, giving me a boost in self-love.

6. I learned I was slacking as a grandfather. Since my session, I have stepped it up and am now enjoying my grandchildren more than ever. I love being a grandpa.

7. I had moments with my father, mother, and brother who are already in Heaven and saw they are doing well.

8. I felt the presence of important people in my current life, realizing that they are all part of my soul group.

9. The feeling of merging with the part of myself that resides in Heaven was an experience in itself. It's hard to put in words, but I felt wise and all-knowing. I felt whole. When I listen to my recording of my session, I hear myself coaching myself.

10. The womb experience was surreal. Feeling my mother's emotional state helped me to know her more than when she was alive. I will never forget that.

11. I appreciated being shown how to get inspiration for composing new songs. I have already written six songs since then.

12. They confirmed that humor is essential in my life and that there may still be opportunities for me to perform. After hearing that, I approached the head trainer and volunteered to do a show at the graduation party. It had been two years since I had performed and was surprised at how I was able to write a whole new routine in just a few hours. People laughed so hard I began to cry. I realized I miss performing and plan to keep it in my life. I also just got permission to rejoin the Screen Actors Guild so I can occasionally audition for movie and commercial roles in San Francisco. That will help balance out my life.

There were various other valuable aspects of my session.

One was experiencing a whole new realm of reality where physics was totally different than here on Earth. I experienced telepathy and found it be as natural as speaking on Earth. When I was Celius in the past life, there were moments when I felt myself in his body and mind. I understood his justification for hanging those poor souls and his regret and sorrow later in life for what he had done.

I now realize that God is omnipotent and far bigger than I can imagine. Souls in Heaven feel the "presence" of God stronger than they do here, but He is still somewhere beyond. I'm guessing there are many levels or dimensions of Heaven and hope to find proof of that as we continue the research.

Look how much I learned about myself, my life, and God in just three hours. Imagine what you will learn when you have your experience in Heaven.

Chapter 32

My Life Between Lives Practice

I've been certified now as a Life Between Lives Regressionist facilitating clients journeys' to Heaven. It is certainly the most rewarding and transformative career in my life. The Newton process is flawless and precise, yet flexible. I follow the procedure step-by-step, and, like magic, my clients find themselves in Heaven.

I have the best job in the world, getting to see Heaven again and again through the inner eyes of my clients. I watch as they get answers to their important questions, heal past, and current traumas, receive physical healings, and visit loved ones in Heaven.

I have the profound privilege of witnessing clients conversing with the souls of people who are still alive on Earth and getting clarity on why they're together in this life. It amazes clients when their past pets show up to see them. Most of all, I love seeing them discover and verify why they chose to be born and what their real mission is.

The client I mentioned earlier, whose husband hung himself had a long conversation with him in Heaven. She learned why he did it and got the most sincere, heartfelt apology from him. She witnessed how the benevolent souls in Heaven were helping him deal with what he had done. Knowing that they were helping him recover and taking care of him gave her a sense of peace. She knows what she has to learn from the experience and that they will be together again. Nowhere else is this kind of closure and emotional relief available.

Others received valuable coaching from their guides about how to proceed in their lives and maintain a connection to Heaven. They visited places of higher learning and got tips on how to express themselves through art and music. Some experienced what souls do there for fun. All of them now realize that they are never alone, and their lives have meaning and purpose.

Last week, one of my clients had a conversation with a soul who would soon be her granddaughter. That soul introduced herself as Avery and said she would be born to help my client and her daughter rekindle their estranged relationship. Another client met the soul who would have been her daughter if she hadn't miscarried. These are gifts of a lifetime.

Recently, parents brought their 10-year-old daughter, Candace, to me, hoping I could help her make sense of a past life she felt she had lived. When Candace was three years old, she told her mother that she was not three years old, but 25. She said her name was not Candace, but Margaret and that a man stabbed her to death in the back seat of a car. She was so adamant about it then and for years afterward, her parents felt there must be something to it.

I was hesitant at first about doing a session for someone so young, fearing that the child might be physiologically harmed by reliving a traumatic event from a past life. After interviewing her, I was convinced that she was prepared. I told her that if things started to get too intense, I would have her leave that body and view it from afar. It would be like watching a movie.

She went quickly into trance and into a past life. It wasn't the life we had hoped for, but still very interesting. In that life, she was a man named Henry. He recalled how shy he was at a high school dance where he met a young girl. A few years later, they married, and he described being at the hospital when his daughter was born. He relived his sadness when his wife died later on in that life and also when he died at age 92. He left that body and was reunited with his wife in Heaven.

This young girl's Guardian Angel appeared, and we were able to ask questions about the life Candace remembered when she was three. We learned that, indeed, she was killed in the back seat of a car in Europe in the late 1940s. The Angel said there was no reason for her to fear anything because that was all in her past. She found out the reason she was murdered and that the person who killed her would also come into her current life when she was older. He was coming back in this life to make it up to her. I could see the relief in Candace's face after the session. She said she was relieved that she didn't have to carry that trauma any longer.

I have been experiencing how emotionally exhausting this work can be. Last week I did three LBL within a few days. After the last session, exhausted and spent, I plopped down on my bed with my clothes on and didn't wake up until 16 hours later. I am learning to pace myself and incorporate the four things that my guide suggested doing to keep from weakening my immune system.

Chapter 33
Heavenly Discoveries

For over 40 years, the Newton Institute has been researching what happens to people when they die and where they go between lives. It started accidentally when a client of Dr. Newton's didn't want to come out of hypnosis because she wanted to "go home" to visit her friends. When Dr. Newton told her to go there, she went to Heaven, where her friends were. He was astonished and skeptical at first. This client seemed to experience something real and meaningful in her deep hypnotic state. His curiosity got the best of him, and he started researching the possibility that when a person reaches a deep state of hypnosis, they have access to what he terms a super-conscious state, where memories of past lives and being in Heaven are stored.

Having a researcher's aptitude and drive, he began serious investigation into this phenomenon. His hunch was correct because over 7,000 more clients reached this deep state and experienced Heaven.

In 2002, Dr. Newton founded the Newton Institute to train other therapists in his techniques and protocol to keep the work and research alive. As of 2020, the Institute has trained and certified about 250 therapists in over 40 countries. Dr. Newton passed away in 2016, and the Institute is carrying on the research that he started.

You can learn more by reading case histories published by Dr. Newton and other researchers from the Newton Institute. A complete list of books follows.

The Validity of the Research

For research to be scientifically valid, researchers must be able to replicate the same test over and over with the same results to prove a hypothesis. The work is then peer-reviewed and finally accepted by the scientific community.

All of us at the Newton Institute are doing metaphysical research using the same criteria as scientific research. We have validated the information below from over 50,000 thousand Life Between Lives sessions with clients all over the world.

Now, it will be up to you whether you accept it. Logic would say that we have proven that Heaven exists and documented what happens when the soul leaves the body. We've discovered the different places in Heaven where souls go. We now know that souls have one life and live that life incarnating time after time into different bodies. Each incarnation provides them with experiences necessary to become more selfless and loving beings. Research has shown us that Heaven is a place of love and benevolence, just as we've always thought it was.

What We Know so Far

It is still shocking to me to see how easy it is for most of my clients to have a successful Life Between Lives experience. About 80% can reach the depth of relaxation needed to visit Heaven. For some of them, it takes two sessions. The other 20% are just not capable of quieting their minds enough to let it happen. Not everyone is initially hypnotizable.

The process can last from three to five hours. When clients reach Heaven, they can be like a kid in a candy store. The guides in Heaven seem to know just what the clients need. They take them on tour, going from station to station having experiences with many souls, and getting their questions answered along the way. At some point, they either know, or the guide indicates when it's time for the facilitator to bring them back to the awakened state.

The Seven Stations that LBL Clients Visit.

Our research is mapping out Heaven. We are discovering more and more all the time. Here are the seven stations we've discovered. There are probably more, but this is what we have so far. Not everyone goes to all seven. Most average three or four in one session.

The Soul Group

Every soul is a part of a soul group who has been together for a long time. I think of it like an acting troupe. They help each other advance by playing characters in each other's lives. When one production is complete, they decide on another play and change roles. That means that someone could be a husband in one life and the wife in another. Or, your child in this life may have been your mother, father, sister or coworker in another. When you think about it from our limited human perspective, it is hard to comprehend, but when you experience a Life Between Lives session for yourself, it makes more sense.

My clients had very rich and loving experiences when they visited their soul groups, especially when they communicated with loved ones already in Heaven.

The Council of Elders

Almost everyone who has an LBL experience finds themselves before the Council of Elders. They may experience from three to 12 or more Elders in a comfortable court-like setting. These loving and benevolent beings are there to guide and support you in your spiritual development.

The Elders are most interested in is your spiritual progress. They are not there to judge you harshly or dole out punishment. Nobody falls through a trapdoor into a fiery furnace. They help you evaluate the past life you just experienced and any current life's problems.

Before your session, your therapist will ask you to compose a list of questions pertaining to your current life. When you are before the council of Elders, your therapist will keep you on track and remind you of the questions you wanted to ask.

Without exception, all of my clients so far have had most of their questions answered to their satisfaction. Occasionally, the Elders will say that they know the answer, but that the client needs to figure it out for their personal growth and development.

The Elders may ask, "What could you have done better in that life"? Or, how do you think you did in that life? Or, what goals did you reach, and what goals didn't you accomplish? It's like having a panel of life coaches who want nothing more than success for you.

The Library

This station contains imprints from everything you have ever done in every life. The research you can do here is unlimited.

Next Life Selection Room

An amazing place where a soul chooses an appropriate body and location for its next incarnation.

Places of Recreation

Heaven, as you would expect, is all about love and joy, and the souls here have lots of fun activities.

The Place of Rejuvenation

Many of my clients experience this place, and it's one of the highlights of the LBL experience. Locations are different but similar for each client. It helps them recuperate from the past lives they just experienced and prepares them for returning home to Heaven.

Here are a few examples of clients' experiences in the place of rejuvenation.

Regan: What do you see in this place?

Client: Oh my god, I'm enveloped in beautiful soft, multi-colored lights. Each carrying different healing properties. It's safe and warm here. I see my body is made up of millions of particles. They look like little soft shiny beads. This energy is cleaning and healing each and every particle of my being.

Another client was floating in a healing pond.

Client: Oh wow, I'm floating in this beautiful pond under a waterfall. It feels amazing. I don't want to leave this place.

Sometimes they receive physical healing of their current body. One of my clients came to me because he was having over 20 seizures per day. He felt repressed memories of his childhood might be the cause. Doctors had done everything they could to no avail.

Regan: Where are you now?

Client: My guide said it would be good for me to come to this place of healing and rejuvenation. I see a giant tree in front of me. It's hard to describe, maybe the closest thing on Earth is a giant redwood or huge oak tree.

Regan: Ask your guide on what to do.

Client: My guide says sit with my back against the tree. ...... Wow, it's beautiful, a rainbow of colored energy is flowing through me. I want to stay here!

A few months later, this client sent me a picture he had drawn of the tree. It's hung on his wall to remind him of the experience. The good news is that his seizures have diminished significantly.

Here is one last example.

The client's guide took her to a place of healing. Instantly she found herself in a soothing desert. The interesting thing was she was face-to-face with Ruth, the woman who she was in the past life that she had just experienced. Both of her selves were now in this place of healing. Her guide had them lie down next to each other, and the healing began.

Client: I can feel the powerful energy of the warm sand, leaching out all of my emotional pain from my body. I'm holding Ruth's hand (the woman who she was in another lifetime).

After some time, I asked:

Regan: Tell me what is happening.

Client: I'm done, but I need to stay with Ruth. I'm still holding and comforting her.

A few minutes later, she told me they were both a lot better. From there, her guide took her to her soul group, where she could have conversations with her father and her sister, who had died in her current life.

The Place of Higher Learning

This station appears to clients in various ways, which are always similar. They describe it as a large university with many classrooms and study areas. They describe this as a happy place where souls can learn all kinds of things. Here is an example from one of my clients.

Regan: What do you see now?

Client: I'm in a beautiful building with lots of rooms. I think it is a place of learning.

Regan: Pick a room and go into it and tell me what's happening?

Client: They're all at desks writing something.

Regan: Go closer and tell me what they are writing.

Client: I can't read it. It looks something like Chinese characters.

Regan: Ask a student what they are writing.

Client: The student just said, "Out of the box," and then turned back to writing.

Her guide then stepped in and asked her if she would like to try writing. She said sure and sat down at a desk and wrote.

Regan: What are you writing?

Client: My pen is moving as if I know what I'm writing, (laughing), but I don't have a clue what it says. It's pretty cool.

This is what another client experienced:

We had just asked her guide if she could visit a place that's like a university for art. He nodded yes, and instantly she found herself in a classroom where souls were painting. My client is an artist and was very excited to be there. She asked the teacher how to improve her art back on Earth. The teacher said she is too technical in her approach and needs to paint more from her heart. The teacher told her to paint with the joy of a child.

A Few Things We Found in Our Research

Here is an overview of what we have discovered about Heaven in the last 40 years.

• In our natural state, we are androgynous, energetic beings of light. Souls choose whether to be male or female, depending upon what is best for the mission they've chosen for their next incarnation. Most souls favor one sex over the other, about 76% of the time.

• In the part of Heaven, we discovered, God is known as the "Presence." You don't see Him, Her or It, but you feel the presence. It appears there are other levels of Heaven beyond what we have discovered.

• We live one life with many bodies.

• Souls choose specific lessons they want to accomplish in each life. One client mentioned that her sole purpose incarnating on Earth was to learn patience, and when asked how long she has been learning patience, she said 500 years.

• Souls in Heaven say Earth is a place of accelerated learning and not for the fainthearted. On Earth, they experience emotional and physical obstacles. On some planets, they may only deal with emotional issues, and on others only physical issues. There are millions of other places that souls go to gain experience.

• The character of a person is a compilation of the experiences of all of their lives, combined with the nature and temperament of their current body and mind.

• Each lifetime, a soul learns lessons to help them advance in spiritual knowledge and love. When they reach a certain level, they can choose a role to help others, whether in Heaven or some physical place like Earth. Many become guides and teachers.

• In 40 years of research and over 50,000 sessions, we have found no evidence of a Hell, at least not as most of the world perceives it. In the afterlife, there is only love and light. Is there correction and consequences for the wrongdoings of souls? Yes, but not in the way most of us have been taught. There is no eternal burning in Hell. The soul redeems itself in other ways to learn from the wrongs they've done. Occasionally, a client thinks they see the devil or a hellish being, but when asked to examine this being more closely, they find it an illusion caused by their Earthly conditioning. Once you see through the illusion, the real truth emerges, finding only love exists there. We are continuing the research, but so far, no Hell as we have been conditioned to believe.

• When a soul leaves the physical body, it sometimes lingers for a bit of time to comfort those left behind.

• Souls come into existence in Heaven and have experiences there. The purpose of the soul is to advance in stages. Once a soul attains a certain level of experience, it can incarnate into a body on Earth or another planet or dimension.

• When souls incarnate, they determine how much of their soul energy is needed to accomplish their intended mission, usually around 50% to 60%. Their remaining energy lives in Heaven, making it possible to have conversations with people who are still alive and in your current life.

• During a Life Between Lives session, the client interacts with their guides, the council of elders, and the souls they interact with in many different forms. Sometimes they appear in human form, other times as colorful energy or a combination of the two. Whatever the case, clients in hypnosis recognize them. That is one of the reasons this experience is so believable.

• Not all souls incarnate or come back for another life. Souls always get to choose.

• The color of the soul's energetic body usually indicates the stage of development reached. Michael Newton's book, Destiny of Souls, goes into detail about this.

• Yes, there are animals in Heaven. Your pets are there. Some of the most meaningful moments of LBL sessions are when clients see their beloved pets again.

Chapter 34
What About You, Are You Curious?

Now that you know that you have a God switch and can take a trip to Heaven, are you inspired to do so? Follow your intuition. If you're meant to have this experience, you will. At this writing, there are around 250 certified therapists spread amongst 40 countries who would love to help you take the journey. If you live anywhere in California, I can help you. To reach me visit my website at:

Book Your Life Between Lives Session

www.VisitTheAfterlife.com

ReganForston@yahoo.com

I'm available as a key speaker for your event and can be contacted at:

REGAN FORSTON

PO BOX 1446

ROSS CA 94957

ReganForston@yahoo.com

To find a facilitator outside of California, go to www.NewtonInstitute.org, where you'll find a list of therapists in 40 countries.

Listen to your intuition for what's next for you. We are all on our own individual path. If you want to learn more about the Life Between Lives process, here are some books that are readily available through most book outlets.

Journey of Souls

Destiny of Souls

Memories of the Afterlife

Llewellyn's Little Book of Lives Between Lives

Here are some other great books of interest.

Many Lives Many Masters

> Or any books written by Brian Weiss

Between Death and Life

> Or any books written by Delores Cannon

As For Me

Trusting my inner guidance has led me to an inspiring journey of self-discovery, putting me in the right place at the right time for the lessons I've needed to learn.

My life is exciting and challenging, discovering who I am, where I came from, why I'm on Earth, and how to use my gifts. By following the clues laid out before me, I've traveled to six countries and had many careers. I went from being a paperboy, gas station attendant, and door-to-door salesman to a real estate broker, professional entertainer as a ventriloquist, clown, magician, mime, stilt walker, juggler, fake motivational speaker, corporate comedian, and Hollywood actor. Then, on the other side of the spectrum, a hypnotherapist, author, songwriter, and finally, a Life Between Life Regressionist, my highest purpose.

I look forward to traveling the globe, giving lectures, and educating people on the Life Between Lives process.

Making sense of it All

I had finished this book and sent it to an editor, but felt something was missing to pull this whole experience together. A few hours later, I saw the movie A *Beautiful Day in the Neighborhood* with Tom Hanks cast as Mr. Rodgers.

Just in case you don't know who Mr. Rodgers is, he's considered the most beloved and influential children's' entertainer of all time with a TV show that ran for over 30 years. He's been described as a peaceful warrior who speaks toddler. His slow and steady voice engaged children better than teachers or parents ever could, confirming that they are valued and loveable just the way they are. Through music, puppetry, and special guests, he taught children how to deal with the problematic aspects of life, like divorce, death of a loved one, rejection, and bullies. He is best known for is his authentic kindness, patience, and compassion, not just for children but for everyone he met.

About 30 minutes into the movie, I had an epiphany. This movie is about the power of genuine kindness, patience, and compassion, all the things needed to be a good Life Between Lives therapist. I realized I'm becoming like Mr. Rogers, and that makes me happy. Near the end of the movie, I felt validated, knowing I'm doing what I came down here to do. Thank you, God, and thank you, Mr. Rogers.

Sincerely,

Regan

Made in the USA
Monee, IL
12 October 2024